What People Are Saying

I have often said that the ability to theme a yoga class is one of the key characteristics of teaching with authenticity and significance. Michelle Berman Marchildon gives us a straightforward, no nonsense, no dogma approach to finding your voice and niche in teaching. If you're looking to cultivate presence, confidence and a strong student base as a yoga teacher, this book is a must!
— Amy Ippoliti, co-founder of 90 Monkeys,
the premier online resource for yoga professionals

I recommend this book wholeheartily to yoga teachers everywhere who want down-to-earth, practical guidance for creating and delivering meaningful and authentic themes in their classes. With her characteristic wit, insight and intelligence, Michelle guides new and experienced teachers through the sometimes challenging terrain of bringing virtue to life through *asana*.
— Christina Sell, author of *My Body is a Temple*
and *Yoga from the Inside Out*

Attention yoga teachers! Learning how to teach *asana* is vital, but learning how to inspire students is a gift and a skill that has taken many of us years to refine. Regardless of your experience, read this book if you want to make your yoga classes powerful and transformational. *Theme Weaver* takes the mystery out of theming, and provides a path to make a complicated process attainable for every teacher.
— Desiree Rumbaugh, creator of the *Yoga to the Rescue* DVD series

In her *dharma* dead serious and *hatha* hilarious style, Michelle Marchildon insists that we as yoga teachers embrace the pragmatic and shun the enigmatic. If you don't want to read this book for you, read it for your students!

    – Darren Rhodes, author of *The Yoga Resource eBook*, director of YogaOasis in Tucson, Arizona

If you have longed to deepen the impact you can make as a teacher, then you are holding the key. The best part about becoming a "Theme Weaver" is that you can't help but receive the blessing of the lessons you wish to teach.

    – Heather Peterson, director of West Coast operations for Corepower Yoga

If you suspect that your students wish you would shut the heck up, then this is the book for you! Michelle Marchildon helps yoga teachers put meaning into instruction, and thereby into the body, without the heavy handedness of too much talk. And she'll entertain you while she does it!

    – Bernadette Birney, author of the award-winning blog, *It's About Yoga, Sort of*

I am inspired by Michelle Marchildon's spunk and triumph over adversity. Now she has harnessed those endearing qualities to create a book that helps any yoga teacher access the power of teaching with a theme. This wise, funny and compassionate resource is a must for any yoga teacher's bookshelf.

    – Emma Magenta, director of South Mountain Yoga, South Orange, New Jersey

THEME WEAVER

Connect the Power of Inspiration to Teaching Yoga

Michelle Berman Marchildon

From the Best-selling Author of
Finding More on the Mat:
How I Grew Better, Wiser and Stronger through Yoga

Published by

WILDHORSE VENTURES LLC

Wildhorse Ventures LLC
A Denver, Colorado company committed to producing real voices in yoga and protecting the rights and sanctuaries of animals worldwide.

Email: WildhorseVenturesLLC@gmail.com

ISBN: 978-09848755-1-1
Library of Congress Control Number: 2013930795

Editing: Eliana Caplan
Cover and Interior Design: Nick Zelinger, *www.NZGraphics.com*
Book Shepherd: Judith Briles
Printer: Color House Graphics

Books may be purchased in quantity
by contacting the publisher directly:
WildhorseVenturesLLC@gmail.com.
The author can be reached at *www.YogiMuse.com.*

First Edition

10 9 8 7 6 5 4 3 2 1

1. Health   2. Fitness   3. Yoga   4. Body, Mind, Spirit

Printed in the United States

For Amy Ippoliti,
Who made me a better teacher.

And for Mike,
Who believed in me,
Before I believed in myself.

"There are only two ways to live your life.
One is as though nothing is a miracle.
The other is as though everything is a miracle."
Albert Einstein

Acknowledgments

I want to acknowledge my teachers, especially Amy Ippoliti, who gave me my second chapter in life, and countless more who inspired me on my mat.

My editor, the mighty (and perfectly picky) Eliana Caplan, My Book Shepherd, Editor and Supreme Hand-Holder Extraordinaire Judith Briles, and the most talented, and patient graphic artist ever, Nick Zelinger.

My students: Thank you so much for laughing at my jokes. And thank you for forgiving me if I showed up less than fully prepared the past few years. Being able to teach weekly classes in the midst of writing two books and raising a family shows that "The Other Eight Limbed Path" works!

Most of all, I want to thank my family. Since my first book, *Finding More on the Mat*, Mike has learned to cook, and my boys, Sam and Teddy, have learned to do laundry. I love you guys. I am not going to thank Lucy and Ricky, our dogs, because they really weren't productive in this process. Maisy, the best dog I ever accompanied here on Earth left us, but I know she was with me in spirit nevertheless.

Lastly, I want to acknowledge the education I received years ago from The Columbia University School of Journalism. The practice of journalism today is changing faster than you can upload a file to the Internet, but people are reading more than ever. Who would have known that the training I received and the experience I had as a working journalist would help me to be a better yoga teacher? However, the point of the journey is not always to know where we are going, but to acquire the skills we'll need when we get there. I was well prepared to arrive. Thank you.

Namaste.

Table of Contents

You Make the Difference

I have a vested interest in creating better yoga teachers: I want to take better yoga classes.

Most yoga classes involve some kind of stretching, strengthening and breath work. And many also involve a theme. In fact, some would say that unless a class has a theme tied to a higher purpose in life, then it is not yoga. It's just exercise. While the poses can change your body, the theme can change your life.

Years ago a bad back brought me to yoga, but that is not why I stayed. Pain is not why anyone stays. We stay because yoga makes us better, from the inside out. In my case, I healed a broken heart. I also revived my career after taking a break from writing professionally for 25 years. I owe this transformation to the yoga teachers who inspired and encouraged me on my mat.

Before I go any further, let me be clear: If you are a yoga teacher, there is no rule that says you have to theme your yoga class. Really. If you have never themed your yoga class and consistently have a full room of students, then by all means toss this book, get a latte or a chai, and call it a day. The *asana*, or yoga poses, are transformational on their own.

On the other hand, this book is for you if you have something to say and are looking for ways to say it clearly and concisely. Or if you had a teacher who changed your life with the subtle way he wove a theme and matched your perspiration with inspiration. If yoga ever changed you, and you want to do the same for others, then keep reading!

Becoming a more inspiring teacher is also a way to differentiate your class from the hundreds of other yoga classes being offered at any given time. Where I live yoga has become something of a commodity and there are as many yoga studios as Starbucks. Teachers compete for students not just with other teachers, *but with every other thing a student can do with an hour of their time.* We are a busy world. To get students into your room, you have to be better than all the other possible options.

The best instructors are the ones who help us realize our potential as well as our poses. After all, any gym teacher can ask you to touch your toes, but yoga is about finding more on the mat. So how do we do this? How do we inspire on the days when we don't feel inspired?

If you want to theme but didn't excel at English or Creative Writing, don't worry. You can learn these skills. Passion is the most important ingredient to good theming and teaching. I can teach you the rest. I have been a writer for nearly 40 years so weaving a theme comes naturally to me. Now it is my *dharma*, or duty, to share it.

The goal as a "Theme Weaver" is to intertwine a theme through the pose sequence without disrupting the yoga. Less is more! We want to add depth without distraction. The best instructors still let the *asana* take center stage.

I am here to serve you, to take the mystery out of great themes, to put confidence in your voice and the weight in your seat at the front of the room. So grab a pen and paper and find an afternoon to invest in yourself. I promise this will change your teaching. Then I hope to take your class.

Namaste.

Chapter One

Understand Your Mission

"Your work is to discover your work and then,
With all your heart, to give yourself to it."
~ Buddha

Who are you?

Did you ever once ask yourself who you are along the way to becoming a yoga teacher? It was probably one of the most important questions you could have considered as you discovered this ancient practice that transforms lives.

For many of us, becoming a yoga teacher might have been a random act. Perhaps we fell in love with the practice, or it simply improved our physical health. From there, we decided to take a teacher training course. Then one day we found ourselves sitting in front of a room of eager students. Awesome! Now what?

In the beginning it might have been easy. You had a lot to say and countless new and creative ideas. Everyone loved your teaching, and you enjoyed sharing all the cool things you just learned about yoga. *OMG! Did you know that the action of the legs can heal your back? OMG!*

I know. I've been there too. It's the most super fun job in the world, until you wake up and can't think of a thing to say, or a new concept to teach, and you hit the wall.

Like a love affair,
Teaching yoga is good, until the day when it is not.

"There are some days where the last thing I want to do is teach yoga," said a veteran teacher I know. "I haven't got any idea what to teach, or what to say, or even why I'm there in the first place."

This book is for that day.

Inspiration is Fickle

Coming up empty in the inspiration department will happen to all of us at some time or another. It doesn't matter if you've been teaching for 20 years or 20 minutes. *Cit* (or reality) happens! But just like yoga, our practice doesn't begin when the pose is easy. It begins when it gets hard. So, welcome to your practice of teaching yoga!

Yoga is a process. It takes time to develop our *asana*, and it takes time to cultivate our understanding of all the layers of philosophy and beliefs. And just like yoga:

Teaching is a practice too.

You will not become a great teacher overnight. This was particularly hard for me because I had always been good at most things I tried, and I was not automatically good at teaching yoga. It takes time to develop our voice and our teaching skills. It takes time to understand who we are and our most effective message.

There will be days when your students applaud. And then there will be days when your class is as inspiring as a rotten tomato. Get over not being perfect. Our work is to discover and learn from the days when we fail.

Teaching the *asana*, or the poses, is often straightforward. You can memorize some great class sequences. You can also rely on a few poses that you can teach in a New York minute.

But a theme is trickier to illuminate because the theme comes from the heart, the authentic "you." Nobody ever came up to me after class and said, "Wow, touching my toes today changed my life." Nobody. Not once.

But I do hear this on occasion:

- "I really needed to hear your message today."

- "I was feeling kind of low, and now I feel better."

- "I am facing something difficult, and your words have given me courage."

- "When I come to your class, I feel good for the whole week."

- "I don't know what I'd do without you." (I made that last one up.)

We teach yoga because we can transform students and change lives. For me, yoga is only a little bit about the *asana*, but it is a lot about how I feel when I practice. And most of that has to do with the theme of the class and the passion of the teacher. And that, my friends, does not come without real work.

Before you can become a great yoga teacher, you need to understand why you became a teacher in the first place. To inspire others, you need to be inspired and feel passionate about your mission.

So I ask again: *Who are you?*

Finding Your Theme

Most of us can teach yoga adequately. We can say the names of the postures, "inhale" and "exhale," and guide students through a safe sequence. In fact, a yoga studio could save the money they pay instructors and just pipe in a recorded yoga class to play for the students. But they don't for one reason: That's not very inspiring. You know what's inspiring? You!

You have a choice: You can be an adequate yoga teacher, or you can be an inspiring, kick-*asana* teacher!

Chances are you did not get into teaching yoga for those entry-level paychecks. You probably had a transformational experience and wanted to share that with others. Right? But how?

Show Me a Theme!

Many of you might be tempted to turn to the part in this book where I give you some themes. I get it. I have very little time too. Let me spare you the agony of studying, contemplating, growing, improving, possibly failing and improving some more. Here are two great themes: "Arrive" and "Journey." The Appendices also list a few more.

However, this book is not about giving you a theme. It is about helping you to create your *own* themes which come *from your heart.* And that involves real effort. There is no getting around it:

Teaching might be fun,
But to be good at it takes work.

The first step to finding a theme, whether you want to use it for the day, or the week, or for a year as do many international travelling yoga teachers, is to figure out the main theme for your life.

You will have a much better idea of what to talk about,
If you know what you are about.

Focus on You

Yoga schools are generally very good at teaching yoga. They can teach us how to work the body in a safe manner. They teach anatomy and terminology. They teach us how to pace, sequence and speak in the active voice. They teach us the Sanskrit names for poses, even if we cannot say them correctly.

But when we get to the theme, the schools throw us into the deep end of the pool without a life jacket. It's not their fault. Teaching how to theme is like teaching how to write; partly it's a gift and partly it's a skill. And the first thing that has to happen is instead of focusing on yoga, you need to focus on you.

Almost anyone can teach a yoga class. But no one, absolutely not one single person, could teach a yoga class exactly like you, *because you make the difference for your students.* Students will show up for you, so now you need to show up for them.

So why did you decide to teach? What is your main message?

Grab Your Pencil

To figure this out, let's start by creating three statements that clarify who you are, and why you teach.* If you know this through and through, it will be the first step to finding consistently authentic themes for your classes and being the teacher you were meant to be.

You will create:

1. A Yoga Bio
2. A Mission Statement
3. Your Yoga Branding

1. The Yoga Bio

The Yoga Bio is a paragraph that functions like a resume. It lists our skills and experience, and we use it to get a job. But unlike a regular resume where we list all the jobs we had since birth, the Yoga Bio should speak only to the experience that influenced your teaching.

I use my Yoga Bio as a description of who I am when I publish my columns and blogs. I also use it partly as the basis for my class description (although I supplement it with my Mission Statement and Yoga Branding, more on that later). And I use it when I publish books (see the inside cover).

Your bio should include:

- What kind of yoga you teach.
- Your years of practicing and teaching experience.

---

* Yoga schools may call them "yoga resumes". I am organizing these statements into classifications for clarity.

- The teachers who influenced you. This guides students to your style.
- Your certifications, if relevant.
- A brief description of your class.

A Sample Yoga Bio

"Jane Doe teaches Ashtanga yoga with an emphasis on finding ease in movement. She has been practicing yoga since 1995 and teaching since 2000. She is a RYT 200 with Yoga Alliance after receiving her training from Sri K. Pattabhi Jois in 1999. Since then, she has been influenced by teachers outside of the Ashtanga School including Baron Baptiste and Shiva Rea. Her classes bring movement into the Ashtanga sequence to allow for creativity in the flow."

What do we know about Jane Doe? She has been teaching and practicing for a long time and therefore conveys a feeling of being experienced. She started with a traditional practice, but has been influenced lately by more of a Power/Vinyasa style. She encourages creativity. In just one paragraph, you understand what she teaches.

The Yoga Bio could suffice as a description for classes at a studio. It could be used to describe a class on a video or in a blog. The Yoga Bio simply states your credentials and what you teach.

When you prepare your Yoga Bio, consider what may be relevant to you and your audience. For example, if you have been teaching for 20 years and have an established student base, then there is no need to list your certifications and credentials. On the other hand, if you are just starting out you might want to mention your training to earn your students' trust. My earliest Yoga Bio listed all the hours and teachers I studied with because truthfully, I probably didn't know what I was doing yet.

The Yoga Bio Format

Here is a format for a standard bio. You can vary it, of course, but you will want to include this basic information so students can easily comprehend what you teach:

> "<u>YOUR NAME</u> has been teaching <u>WHAT KIND OF YOGA</u> for <u>HOW MANY YEARS</u> and practicing for <u>NO. OF YEARS.</u> (We include the practice years because we learn as much from our practice as we do from our teaching, and students know it.) <u>YOUR NAME</u> was inspired by <u>YOUR INSPIRATION</u> and also studied with <u>YOUR TEACHERS</u>. (Always list the teachers whose style inspired you, and who you wish to emulate). <u>YOUR NAME</u> graduated from a <u>200/500 hrs TT</u> in <u>YEAR</u>. List any other certifications if relevant, such as therapeutics, or level two trainings. <u>YOUR NAME</u> teaches a class with <u>BRIEF DESCRIPTION</u>. This part is important as students want to know do you teach with music, high, low or no heat, alignment, slow tempo, gentle, physical, humor or compassion. Keep it brief, but give them an idea of what to expect."

The Yoga Bio tells people *what you teach*. The next step, the Mission Statement, tells them *why you teach*. This is where you describe what makes your offering unique in the yoga world.

2. The Mission Statement

A Mission Statement lets the world know why you teach yoga. Obviously, if you don't know, then this will be difficult to complete. But it is a critical step to discovering your unique offering and voice.

A Mission Statement may be a sentence or a paragraph that focuses your teaching and defines your market. If you look at the Yoga Bio above, it does not state why Jane Doe became a teacher. You can't get a sense of who she is, or what she's about. If you decide to go to her class, it will be because you are looking for the Ashtanga sequence with a little creative flair. And believe me, there are a lot of Ashtanga teachers in the world today, so you will want to differentiate yourself so students can find "you!"

By being clear about your mission, you will understand which students you serve best. Then you can choose the studios and locations with the students who will most likely be a good fit. This saves a lot of your valuable time, and helps you make more money with more mats in your room. Booyah!

A Mission Statement achieves the following:

- It will focus your message and define your unique offering.

- It will remind you why you teach when you can't remember.

- It will appeal to your market, and your market will find you.

A Sample Mission Statement

"When Ashley was a child, she survived a car accident that left her with a broken back and a year of rehabilitation. Since then, her passion has been to help others find more peace in their bodies and patience in their heart on the road to healing. She discovered yoga in 2002 and has used an approach combining alignment and surrender to find a compassionate path to restoring health. Her goal is to welcome everyone to the mat so they may rediscover wellness through a gentle practice."

What can you tell from this Mission Statement? The teacher is nurturing and compassionate. She offers a gentle practice with alignment and an emphasis on healing. If you are looking for a rock and roll Vinyasa class, this is probably not it. If you are looking for the Ashtanga sequence, *forggedaboudit*. But if you are looking for a moderate, restorative practice, come on in.

Your Mission Statement is a way to advertise truthfully so the right students can find you. The last thing you want is false advertising. I used to teach a style of yoga that was alignment-oriented, but its corporate literature described it as: "Stepping into the flow of Grace." I cannot tell you how many students would show up because they wanted to "flow." But it was not necessarily a "flow" style of yoga. No matter how good the class was, those students were going to be disappointed because they wanted something else.

A strong Mission Statement
Will attract students aligned with your offering,
And who resonate with your message.

Awesome Mission Statements

Corporate America has long used a Mission Statement to direct their workers toward the same objective. You can find a company's mission on its website. It is the same for large-scale corporate yoga studios and most famous yoga teachers. Perhaps the reason famous teachers became famous, is because they knew exactly why they were teaching, and their students found them?

Below are a few yoga Mission Statements I admire for their clearly stated purpose and originality. Notice that each one creates a unique perception of the studio or teacher.

Corepower Yoga

"Corepower Yoga strives to increase awareness and widespread adoption of yoga by making yoga accessible to everyone, through a variety of yoga styles, for beginners and more advanced yoga students, and class times to meet any schedule."

Interpretation: Through the words *widespread, accessible, everyone, beginners* and *more advanced* (as in, not totally advanced) one understands that the yoga will be manageable for most students.

YogaWorks

"At YogaWorks, we believe Yoga is for everyone. It is our mission to honor and embrace each student's search for personal growth,

13

wellbeing, and fulfillment by offering the highest quality yoga programs to people of all ages and from all walks of life. We do this with love, compassion, a sense of humor, and with respect for what each individual can accomplish through Yoga and throughout their lives."

Interpretation: Yoga for everyone, incorporating quality and compassion. YogaWorks also states that every teacher has a RYT 500 status with Yoga Alliance, which creates the impression of experience.

Omtime Yoga, Boulder, Colorado

"Born out of a love for deep transformation, we strive to meet students where they ARE, and carry them forward into where and WHO they want to be."

Interpretation: This studio helps students grow body and soul.

Livia Shapiro, Boulder, Colorado

"I believe the human spirit is meant to be wild and free and I aim to re-wild the body, mind, and heart through the practices of yoga, dance, and authentic connection. To continually show up is an aim not to be taken lightly or for granted. And so we practice… in ecstasy."

Interpretation: This class is going to rock and you may get stuck with yo' head up yo' *ass-ana.*

Sacredi, Denver, Colorado

"A family-oriented community studio and boutique in the heart of Park Hill. Our instructors are individually celebrated in the yoga

community as some of the most experienced, extensively trained, and highly sought after instructors—anywhere!"

Interpretation: Family oriented! Come get your community on! There will be classes for grandparents, moms, dads, and kids, and the instructors are excellent.

Christina Sell, Austin, Texas

"Christina Sell is dedicated to helping people of all ages and abilities experience the joys of yoga practice and conscious living."

Interpretation: Everyone welcome, with a focus on awareness.

School of Yoga, Christina Sell and Darren Rhoades

"The School of Yoga offers educational programs that connect people to the healing power of the Heart's Light through traditional spiritual teachings, disciplined yogic practices and the transformational power of community. Inspired by the lineage of Western Baul Master, Lee Lozowick, the School of Yoga is dedicated to authentic spirituality and practical work on self."

Interpretation: "Practical work on self" indicates the journey will also be inward.

Elle Potter, St. Louis, MO

"Bring a sense of laughter and adventure to everything we do."

Interpretation: You will have fun and not take yourself too seriously.

The Mission Statement – Outward Bound

Once you have created your Yoga Bio and Mission Statement, you can blend the two to create a kind of yoga movie trailer showing a preview of your class. The purpose is to attract the right students for you. Filling the room with students who are looking for something else will not serve you, or them. I would rather have six students whose lives I can transform than a room of 30 students who think I am a blathering idiot.

In my case, my Yoga Bio and Mission Statement both talk about my interest in using alignment to find a deeper experience on the mat. I am not interested in teaching classes where the students dance their way through yoga (Not that there's anything wrong with that; it's just not me). Nevertheless, every now and then someone will come to my class who asks for it to be "hot and hard." I'm thinking, "Did you see the trailer? I am not your teacher." I might introduce them to a teacher who is a perfect fit, and they are both usually grateful for the guidance. In this way, the student is not turned off of yoga, and may revisit your offering sometime in the future.

Define your Mission Statement clearly and your students will find you, and better yet, they will stay with you year after delightful year.

The Mission Statement – Inward Bound

While your Mission Statement can describe your style so students can find you, it can also be used as a tool to go inward and figure out who you are. If you know exactly who you are, and why you are teaching, then it will be easier to find your themes.

The single most important thing that distinguishes an inspiring teacher is the passion they feel about the subject. You know how you feel when a teacher is on fire? That's how you want to be for your students too. Passion is contagious.

But it's not always easy to feel the spark. For example, have you ever had a busy day and then had to step into a room and begin teaching? Sometimes I have to get my kids to school, and then make a killer drive to a studio only to deal with a broken toilet and a frozen computer before I teach. It makes it hard to focus on inspiration.

On those days, a strong Mission Statement will remind you why wanted to do this in the first place. Right before I teach, I take out my Mission Statement and read it calmly to myself. This only takes a few seconds, and I remember why on Earth I thought I could be a yoga teacher when I can barely check in the class. It reminds me that I am here to change lives and to help people find more of what they want. That gets me going again.

"Truthfully," said one yogi who took a year off from teaching, "Not teaching from my honest mission statement is what killed me from wanting to teach."

Creating Your Mission Statement

Creating your Mission Statement takes work, and if it can improve your teaching and provide the basis for your financial security, then you might want to consult a professional. For example, a fashion model (or many of the rest of us) would not ever cut her own hair or take her own publicity photos. So why would you create your own Mission Statement? This might be a good time to hire a professional.

There are professionals in the market today who are there to help you with marketing, mission statements, yoga branding, colors, the fonts you use to express yourself and your website. They will help you focus on just about everything you are trying to communicate, so you will be more of you and attract more students. A consultant will help you figure out what you are about.

One consultant I know specific to yoga and to finding your unique expression is Jessica Boylston-Fagonde and her company, *BrandThyself.com*. She has a therapeutic approach to understanding your purpose, and then adding that to yoga. By focusing on "personal branding," Jessica identifies your strengths, attributes, and qualities so you can express that to others on all of your materials. She is also a yoga teacher, so she understands our business.

However, if you cannot afford a consultant at this time, then grab a pencil to get started. Introspection and contemplation is the key.

Ask yourself these questions:

- Why do I love yoga?
- Why did I first get on the mat?
- Why did I stay?
- What inspired me to be a teacher?

Consider the following:

- Who are my favorite teachers? We gravitate toward certain people because they embody some element of who we want to be. Figure out what that is.

- Who are my students? Who do I want to teach? Ask them what they like about your teaching to discover your strengths. Just as we cannot see our face without a mirror, we often cannot see our gifts. So ask those around you for reflection.

- What poses do I like to practice? The poses we avoid may have more answers about who we are than the poses we rock.

- What is my overall message? If you are here to serve, then who can you serve best? And equally important, who do you not serve as well?

A great Mission Statement is self-reflection, self-promotion and purpose all in one. It will be your true north, when you are lost. It will guide you, and guide students to you, and serve as the foundation for choosing your themes. You cannot spend too much time creating and pondering your Mission Statement. Don't worry if it's not perfect; you will revise it as you evolve over time.

3. The Yoga Brand

Now that you have a Yoga Bio and Mission Statement you are ready to consider the third message and that is your unique "Yoga Brand." This is how you differentiate your offering from everyone else, and sum up who you are and why you teach.

This concept of a "Yoga Brand" is not about what kind of yoga that you teach, for example, a Bikram or Iyengar style. It is about *your unique message* in teaching yoga. That is "*Your Yoga Brand.*"

The Yoga Brand boils down your message *to just a few key words that define exactly what you are about when you teach yoga.*

19

This becomes very important when we start to theme. The more you know what motivated you, the easier it will be to inspire others. Yoga branding is more than just another *"who am I"* exercise. It's a way to distill your message into a few powerful words for inspiration.

Think of the Yoga Brand as the answer to the following equation, which was created by Jessica Boylston-Fagonde:

You + Yoga = Your Unique Yoga Brand.

Yoga branding is like a fingerprint; it is unique, distinctive and looks different to different people. Here are some examples of why people teach, and what their "brand" may sound like after they asked themselves, "What is my main message when I teach yoga?"

Awesome Yoga Brands

I teach because I want students to…
- Find more on the mat, to find more out of life.
- Feel worthy of greatness.
- Heal physically and spiritually.
- Connect to a larger purpose.
- Find peace in our busy lives.
- Know they are loved.
- Know fear is stronger than love.
- Feel accepted and good enough as we are.

Just as no two yogis will ever be exactly alike, no two Yoga Brands will ever be exactly alike. We each bring our unique reasons for teaching to our classes, and that will be reflected in the Yoga Brand we use to express ourselves, and the themes we choose to communicate. If you cannot afford a professional (although getting help is often much less expensive than making a mistake on all your materials and correcting it down the line), then do this on your own. It is one thing not to pay a professional, *but under no circumstances can you afford not to do this work for yourself.*

Focus on Your Unique Message with a Friend

1. Get a friend and sit together facing each other. You will need a pencil and two pieces of paper.

2. On one piece of paper take 15 minutes to write down a couple of paragraphs saying why you teach. Your Mission Statement will help.

3. One at a time, face each other and read your list out loud for ten full minutes saying, "I teach yoga because…" Your friend will write your answers on the second piece of paper. You must continually speak about yourself and yoga the whole time. It is important that you do not shut up! Keep talking even when you run out of things to say, and then say whatever comes into your head. That is when it gets good.

4. Your friend will write down the words and catch phrases that you repeat.

5. At the end of the exercise, read the list of repeated words and phrases to your friend and give her the paper. This forms the basis for your Yoga Branding and Mission Statement.

I did this exercise talking to myself in a mirror because I was on a deadline and there were no friends around, except for my dogs and husband, and I wouldn't call either of them useful to me for branding, or even good listeners. I came up with the following words:

> *Yoga, Yogi, Writer, Mother, Funny, Laughter, Resilient,*
> *Finding More, Finding Love, Finding Happiness,*
> *Finding My Inner Badass,*
> *Joyful, Pimple* (that was what I saw in the mirror)

I became the "Yogi, Mother, Muse" which I shortened to "The Yogi Muse." I use the phrase "Finding More on the Mat" for branding because I am all about people re-discovering their potential. Furthermore, my editor came up with: "The Erma Bombeck of the Mat." I LOVE this because she was my idol. How sweet when you discover that you have become an aspect of a person you admire, and Erma Bombeck was a muse for me.

In addition to "The Yogi Muse," my 'branding' includes certain colors on my website, blog and communications. I have chosen a font that is whimsical and pictures that convey both my family and fearlessness in yoga. That pretty much sums me up.

A Word of Caution

While great branding can manifest your mission with just a couple of words, it can also get you way off track. Try to work with someone who knows you, who knows yoga and who knows marketing. I have a quite a few yogi friends who went through branding and came out without their clothes on! Do not pose in your underwear on your website unless that is what you are really selling. Balance the need to be provocative with who you are, and how best to serve your students. If you are a mother and most of your students are other mothers, there is no need to pose nearly nude on your website. If you are an athletic yogi selling a Power Yoga strength-oriented class, you do not have to quote Rumi every ten minutes. Truth in advertising will attract your loyal students.

Vision Provides Clarity

Taking this time to focus on "you" will give you clarity in teaching. Creating a Yoga Bio, a Mission Statement and your Yoga Brand is a chance to explain to others what you hope to accomplish. But it also clarifies things for you! On those days when you have temporarily lost your way, or become misaligned with the world, if you just glance at these statements you will quickly remember why you teach.

No two yoga brands or mission statements are alike because you will have your own unique reasons to teach yoga. Get in touch with who you are and why you teach because it will form the basis for the themes you can rock in the room. It will be your completely unique thumbprint for your class.

Doing this work on ourselves is about being able to give back to our students. Our best efforts enable their best efforts on and off the mat. So take your time, contemplate, and come up with the unique reason why you teach yoga. It will be the reason students come to your class; they want a bigger helping of you.

Finding You

The Mission Statement Worksheet

Contemplate on the following:

Your Teachers:

Who are your favorite teachers?
What do you like about them?
What themes inspire you?
What turns you off?
What makes you want to come back to their class?

Your Students:

Who are your typical students?
How old are they?
Who do you most relate to in your room?
What are they like physically?
What is their practice like?
What type of student is hard to teach?
Why?

Your Practice:

Why did you first come to yoga?
What were you looking for?
Why did you stay?
What poses do you enjoy?

Which ones do you avoid?
What did you find that was unexpected?

Your Teaching:

Why did you become a yoga teacher?
What most surprised you about teaching?
How can you serve your students?

Describe yourself in about a Twitter-size feed,
160 characters or a very small paragraph.
Brevity creates clarity.

Your Mission Statement:

Think of a statement that sums up why you teach and
how you can serve your students. Don't worry if it's not
perfect. It will evolve over time as you change.

Your Unique Yoga Brand:

Sum up your Mission Statement with a phrase that
completes this sentence:

"I teach yoga because ..."
"I teach yoga to ..."

Chapter Two

Choose Your Themes Wisely

"Hard times arouse an instinctive desire for authenticity."
~ Coco Chanel

Years ago in my first yoga teacher training, I was called to the front of the room to lead a segment of the class. Even though I was scared to death, I walked up and took my place.

"Inhaaaaaaaaale," I roared. "Exhaaaaaaaaaale," I bellowed in what I thought was a deep sexy voice, but I probably sounded like a Sasquatch in heat.

"That was nice," my teacher said, "But next time, could you please do it the way Michelle would teach, and not Baron Baptiste."

Right? Michelle who? At that time I had no idea who on Earth I was, or why I was even in yoga teacher training (except it seemed like a good way to get out of making dinner three nights a week). It would take me another year of teaching, studying, practicing, self-reflection, maturity, and confidence to figure it out. But in the beginning, I could only be a poor imitation of who I thought I should be.

"I had no idea that being your authentic self could make me as rich as I've become," said Oprah Winfrey. "If I had, I'd have done it a lot earlier."

There is Only One You!

I was not successful as a yoga teacher until I was me. It was the same for every career I ever had, but never more so than when standing in front of a room full of highly-attuned yogis who could smell a phony from a mile away.

Students show up to see you.
Now all you have to do is show up for them.

Authenticity in our lives is earned the old fashioned way, one day at a time. We live, we learn, we become more of who we were meant to be through the challenges we face.

The number one way to be authentic in your teaching is through your themes. Interestingly, many try. But you are the only you. Others can teach your *asana* sequence; in fact, there are many set sequences of yoga. Others can teach physical yoga actions. But nobody can teach *your* theme exactly like *you.*

The one completely unique aspect to your yoga class is how you inspire your students and the passion you bring to the moment.

Yoga, in many ways, has become a commodity. Where I live there are more studios than Starbucks. I can find a yoga class every 15 minutes, within a 15 minute drive. What's more, I live in a state with 300 days of sunshine a year! So not only do yoga teachers compete with each other, but we also compete with however a person chooses to spend their one free hour of their day (darn that beautiful Colorado weather).

How do you offer something so unique, so indescribably delicious that students will rearrange their schedule so they don't miss a class? You must connect passion to authenticity, which creates not just a class, but an amazing experience.

How to Choose a Theme

The most important question when you begin to plan your classes isn't what should I talk about today, but who am I today? I usually choose an idea because it is of interest to me, or because it speaks to something I've been going through. It must be something that I feel passionate about, or that I at least care about. That way the class sounds honest. Also, chances are my students may be experiencing something similar. For example, I notice that if I feel chaotic, lots of other people do too. This builds a sense of community in the room.

It usually sounds something like this:

> Me: "I've been feeling so out of control lately."
> Student: "*OMG*, me too!"
> Me: "See, we are connected. That is the yoga."

While I am oversimplifying this, it is true that universally we are often connected. If we can tap into whatever is going on, it could lead into a class talking about the universe, or connection, or about how to manage chaos, or how to find peace. The possibilities are endless, but it starts with being real about what you are feeling at that moment.

If you have no idea, try yoga or meditation. Everyone says it works!

Choose Themes because:

- They speak to you.
- They support your Mission Statement.
- You have experience with them.

When Good Themes Go Bad

Good themes can easily go bad in the wrong hands.

The difference between a class which lifts your students up versus a class which brings them down is often your perspective. I cannot tell you how many classes I have been to where the teacher began with something like, "My mother is dying." It's very hard to find an uplifting class from something you haven't yet put into perspective. Remember, your mess is your mess. Your students will have their own messes to clean up on the mat.

Like all people, I have experienced setbacks in life. However, I wasn't immediately ready to talk about them, and certainly not in the yoga room. I had to find a place where I learned to be a better, wiser or stronger person as a result of the experience. Interestingly, I wrote about many of my hardships in my first book, but I wasn't ready to speak about them for another year. It often takes time.

Yoga Teacher Christina Sell, author of *My Body is a Temple* and *Yoga from the Inside Out*, puts it this way:

You need to be in a place where you can offer inspiration,
Before you can talk about it in a class.

Nobody should be opening a vein and bleeding out on our students. There is no set rule about how long this might take; it could be a few days or it could take years before you can share openly about difficulties. But do not do it until you can at least laugh your way to enlightenment. If you are still sobbing into your pillow at night, that's a clue you are not yet ready to bring it to your students. They have their own problems; they don't need yours as well.

A theme is ready when you can provide:

- Experience, which made you better.
- Strength, you can offer to your students.
- Hope, to inspire others.

Another way a good theme can go bad is when it is not yours. For example, there is a teacher in my area who can theme a class around the *chakras* beautifully. She is fascinated by the *chakras*, she studies everything about them, she takes workshops on them, and she could and should probably write a book on them. When I am in her room, she makes my whole body come alive through these energy focal points. Her passion is what carries the theme and changes my practice.

Now, when I try to theme on the *chakras*, it sounds like this:

**"Um, what is the first *chakra* called again?
And isn't it red?"**

Right? It's because the chakra theme is not me. I don't live that theme, so I can't theme that theme. If you don't feel passion for a theme, it's very hard to inspire others with it.

Passion is the key to finding your themes. It doesn't matter what you are passionate about, it is the passion itself which is contagious.

For example, I am deeply inspired by International Yoga Teacher Martin Kirk, who is one of the world's leading experts on anatomy. Even though I am an English major and not an anatomy buff, when you attend his classes and lectures, even the femur bone can make your heart sing. I have been in his room and felt moved to tears by the beauty of my sacrum! But if I try to teach anatomy, it will land like a bag of bones.

We appreciate and admire passion, in whatever form in takes. That is what makes a class inspiring.

Do not choose a theme because:

- It is your favorite teacher's theme.
- It rhymes (but rhyming can be fun too).
- It involves 'letting go,' which someone said was a good thing.

Breaking Down a Class

The hardest part of choosing a theme is deciding who you are and why you wanted to teach. But once you have created your Yoga Bio, Mission Statement and Yoga Branding, you will have a better idea of what you want to talk about. And whatever theme you choose, it will have your unique interpretation. That is why nobody can rock your theme like you can. Nobody.

Now that we know who we are, and what kinds of subjects we might want to talk about, let's start by creating a class which will inspire your students.

The *Theme* and the *HOV*

What does it take to build a successful class theme? It begins with three main concepts:
1. *You*
2. The *Theme*
3. The *HOV*, or *Human Operating Value*

1. *You*

You are the foundation to your themes. Who you are, and why you teach is the secret to being authentic in the room and choosing great topics. By now, I hope you have considered what you are passionate about, and what you like to talk about. This will make it more natural to choose a theme.

2. The *Theme*

A *Theme* is a phrase, or an idiom, or a maxim, or a concept, or an expression that sets up your class. It should speak to you. It should be interesting enough that you can talk about it for an hour or 90 minutes, or even a three hour workshop and not get bored. It should be succinct, life-affirming or inspiring in some way. And it should be generic enough that the majority of your room will be able to relate to it.

Some *Theme* Ideas:
- Keep a beginner's mind.
- Analysis paralysis – when you overthink things.
- Find your courage.
- Stand tall in your truth.
- Something is happening here.

Let's look at the last one in our list, "Something is happening here." This phrase can be used to construct a class around the concept of change and transformation. You could say it in several different ways to encourage students to embrace the positive changes they have made since discovering yoga. However, you must be careful—as with any theme—that your class will sound trite and clichéd if you do not do the work to support it.

How to Construct a Simple *Theme*

Even a simple idea needs work, and the best ideas can go downhill quickly without it. Once you have your main concept, you will need to find supporting statements to use in your class.

If you say the same thing over and over again, i.e., "Something is happening here, something is happening here, something is happening here" your students will probably think you are crazy. They will tune you out. Worse, they may not come back to your class. If you repeat yourself over and over again, your studio might even shut down, then yoga will die and the whole world will suffer. You see how important it is to skillfully construct your theme?

Furthermore, one phrase may not speak to every student, so stating the concept in an altered but similar manner gives you a greater chance of reaching more students. And the more students who understand what you have to say, means more mats in your room and the more lives you can affect positively.

Phrases you might say to support "Something is happening here:"

- The only constant is change.
- Renovation is coming to a body near you.

- Revolution is in the air.
- Find something new by coming to my retreat in Costa Rica.

Creating a class around a phrase is a clear and simple start to theming yoga. If your phrase is powerful enough, it might even produce meaningful transformation in your students. International Yoga Teacher Baron Baptiste has amazing phrases that have made deep and everlasting changes in my practice. I will never forget a class I took with him based on a theme, "Death is coming to a body near you." That phrase made me work harder in the room because I didn't want to be the next body!

However, you may notice that teaching a theme without connecting it to anything meaningful in our lives leaves a little of the "SHAZAM" factor on the table. For example, saying "Something is happening here," without saying what it is, leaves a student feeling empty, like they ate some processed food without any real nutrition.

A *Theme* without meaning will not touch your student's lives or create the foundation for change that yoga can enable. It will leave them full but not nourished. Something may be happening, but what it was it 'ain't' exactly clear!

If you want your students to have a deeper experience, you need to connect your *Theme* to a *Human Operating Value* in your class.

3. *The Human Operating Value* or *HOV*

Even the most clever and original *Themes* will pack a greater punch if they incorporate a *Human Operating Value* in the class. The *Human Operating Value,* or *HOV,* is the part which speaks to making us better people off the mat.

The fact is very few students are perfect. Very few come to the mat because they already know it all. (Although, I know some who think they do.) Most of us come to the mat because we are looking for help, or change, or comfort.

While it's a wonderful form of exercise, yoga keeps our students coming back because it becomes about the inspiration as much as the perspiration.

One purpose of yoga,
Is to provide a hit of inspiration to the day.

While other forms of exercise raise your heartbeat for an hour, yoga is able to change you into a better person for life! That is how we compete with all the other things people can choose to do with their time. A well-chosen, well-spoken, well-crafted theme can rock your student's world. What's more, the extra effort they are motivated to put into practice can give them a better butt. Who can compete with that?

No matter how awesome your idea for a theme is, if it doesn't inspire, then it can fall short of the mark. To inspire, a theme *must be connected to a fundamental quality in humans.* I'm labeling that the *HOV. A Human Operating Value* is the essential quality that makes us better.

When a Theme *is tied to an* HOV,
We become more of who we were meant to be!

Common *HOVs* in yoga include:

Love, Affection, Compassion, Forgiveness, Surrender
Connection, Community, Universal or Divine Love
Acceptance, Confidence, Recognition, Approval
Self-love, Self-care, Self-study, Studentship
Transformation, Change, Renewal, Non-clinging
Strength, Fearlessness, Perseverance, Effort, Courage, *Tapas*

Themes that Fall Short

These are some real life examples of *Themes* I have heard used in a class that, in my opinion, fell short of life-changing because they did not speak to me in any meaningful way. There was no connection to a *Human Operating Value,* and therefore, did not inspire me off the mat. In fact, some of these classes barely inspired me to keep going for 90 minutes.

Banal, Bland and Just Plain Boring Themes

- Caterpillars are cute. Let's crawl around today.
- The Olympics are neat. Let's celebrate the Olympians.
- Let's play upside down because playing is fun.
- I love the ocean, so let's "swim" our warrior poses.
- Let's be a merry band of bohemians! (Really? Because I kind of have a mortgage).

To understand why these examples fall short, let's recall the definition of what makes a *Theme*:

> "A *Theme* *is a phrase, or an idiom, or a maxim, or a concept, or an expression that sets up your class. It should speak to you. It should be interesting enough that you can talk about it for an hour or 90 minutes, or even a three hour workshop and not get bored. It should be succinct, life-affirming or inspiring in some way. And it should be generic enough that the majority of your room will be able to relate to it."*
> AND.... *It should make us better off the mat!*

That's why we want to connect our *Theme* to an *HOV*.

Connecting your *Theme* to an *HOV*

To rock our *Theme* of "Something is happening here," let's connect it with a *Human Operating Value* so the message becomes more meaningful for students. You could choose several *HOV* possibilities such as "dedication," "self-study," or "building community." In this case, we'll tie our *Theme* to "transformation."

Sample phrases for teaching the *Theme* with "transformation":

- Something is happening here.
  Notice you feel different than you did
  50 minutes ago.

- Do you feel the change in your body?
  Do you see the change in your attitude?

- Are you happier? More tolerant? Healthier? Or stronger?

- Something has happened in our lives.
  The transformation begins on our mat,
  and we carry it through to everything we do.

The *Human Operating Value* is a way to refine a *Theme* so it speaks to our fundamental natures. When the class becomes about transformation, it becomes a more inspiring message than simply saying a phrase over and over again. It also reminds students of the benefits of practicing yoga. When the power of inspiration is connected to perspiration, then you have a motivated, rocking yoga class.

Play It Again, and Again Sam

There is nothing like being a local teacher to make you a brilliant teacher. If you have to face the same students every week, or two or three times a week, it will make you versatile with your words. You won't be able to say the same old things every class, because your students will already know your jokes. They will know all your tired sequences.

However, the beauty of the *Theme* and the *HOV* concept is you can mix and match them to create an entire library of material. You can't keep doing the same shtick because people will get bored. But if you choose a refreshing new *Theme* to match with an *HOV* that you like to use, it will keep your classes fresh and your students engaged.

***Themes* or phrases that work with "transformation":**

- Write a new ending to your story.
- The journey creates expansion.
- Yoga is a path to more.
- Who were you meant to be?
- Something is happening here.

By creating five *Themes* that work with "transformation," you have created the opportunity for five distinct classes using the same *Human Operating Value.* If you have contemplated on the value of change and transformation in your life, then you can re-share some of those insights for each class. But each class has a distinct and unique feel to it. Furthermore, if you change the peak yoga posture, your students will have no idea they are receiving the same class with a new spin. The pasta may be the same, but the sauce is new!

Lastly, the opposite is also true which is that if you love your *Theme,* then you can mix it up by expressing it with a new *HOV* and a new meaning for your class.

HOVs that work with the *Theme,* "Something Is Happening Here":

- Transformation and personal change.
- Self-Study, the way you improve yourself.
- Creating community.
- Tapas, finding new discipline and rigor in your practice.
- Hope, emphasizing optimism.

By creating five new *HOVs* that work with "Something is happening here," you have created another five distinct classes! Again, if you have contemplated on what the concept meant in your life, then you can re-share some of those insights for each class.

From your initial effort to create a class around "transformation" and "Something is Happening Here," you now have 10 unique classes you can teach from the same little tidbit of inspiration. This will save you time and energy when you get ready to teach. And, the *Theme* has blossomed from a potentially hackneyed expression to something meaningful in students' lives.

The ability to mix and match *Themes* and *HOVs* becomes a critical skill when you are a local teacher looking for constant sources of inspiration. So many yogis tell me they experience burn out and exhaustion from trying to come up with a fresh new idea for their class every week. Some teachers I know create a new class every day for their students!

To save yourself time and effort, you can recycle your classes and re-use your creative wordings and you will get more energy from less work. Believe me, when you teach "Write a new ending to your story," your students will have very little idea that it is essentially the same class as "Something is happening here." Yet they can both be about the power of transformation in our lives. A lot of your work in creating a new class has already been completed.

Warning! Warning!

Like the robot from the old television show, "Lost in Space," I want to wave my arms wildly here to warn you of a very common mistake when you start to theme in your classes. Do not, and I mean it, DO NOT switch your *Themes* or *HOVs* in the middle of a class as you would switch a horse in the middle of a race. Abraham Lincoln coined this phrase referring to political parties who changed their candidate in the middle of an election. Believe me, it never works!

Here's a poem so you can remember:

"Do not switch horses in the middle of a race.
Do not switch horses, even if you want to save face.
Do not switch horses,
If you care about the quality of your class,
Because instead of riding a winner,
You will instead become the ass."

– Michelle Marchildon

There is nothing more annoying than a teacher who starts talking about "connection" and then brings in "surrender." The same goes for switching your *Themes*. Do not start with the phrase, "Something is happening here" and then start talking about, "Taking responsibility in life." These are different ideas, apples and oranges. Do not do that to your students when they are trying to breathe and practice. It is the result of poor planning, poor focus and poor execution. *OMG, please shoot me if I am in your class and you do this.* Thank you.

Everyone Has a Prevailing *HOV*

Being an effective and authentic yoga teacher is first about knowing yourself. Now that you have written a Mission Statement, and know your Yoga Brand, you will also know the *Themes* and *HOVs* that speak to you. A bad choice will result in an awkward class.

For example, the absolute worst class I ever taught was on the *HOV* of love. Seriously. I was blah blah blahing on how everyone should just feel love, and be love, and I even played some song on choosing love. I wanted to walk out of my own class and hang myself!

This was not authentic to me, since frankly, I find love challenging. So who am I to tell anyone else what to do? I am much better at telling people to have courage and to persevere for more of what they want. Love? Not so much.

When you remember why you decided to teach yoga, you will be able to pick the *Themes* and *HOVs* that work for you. Furthermore, because your message is clear, you will attract like-minded students and have more mats in the room, and resonate with more students. Although I do not like to teach on "love," I do enjoy teachers who can because it is something I want to nurture. And while I am a "badass" yoga teacher, the last class I need to go to would be for empowerment. If I was any more empowered, I'd eat my young.

The list of *Human Operating Values* you feel comfortable with will be somewhat limited and probably tied to your Mission Statement. However, the good news is that there are infinite number of ways and metaphors you could come up with to express those values.

Some of my favorite teachers rock personal *HOVs* like self-acceptance, courage and compassion. However, while they may come back to an essential *HOV*, they rarely, if ever, teach the same exact class. I hope this is starting to make sense.

Choose You!

Finding a *Theme* and an *HOV* is just like yoga. Every time you fail, that is the moment for clarity. Every time you cannot think of something to say, it becomes an opportunity to go deeper into what you are feeling at that moment. Teaching is a practice too. If you can focus on your Mission Statement, you will remember why you teach, and you will remind your students of why they wanted to practice with you as well.

"To be yourself in a world that is constantly trying to make you something else, is the greatest accomplishment."

Ralph Waldo Emerson

Choose Your *Themes* and *HOVs*

You are the only *You*!

What are the main *HOVs* in your Mission Statement?
What are your favorite concepts to teach?
What makes you comfortable and uncomfortable?
Know what you are about, and what you are not about.

What Are Your Strengths?

What is your style in the room, formal or informal?
Do you like to make them laugh? Is your skill holding
the energy?
Are you excellent at keeping the breath and pace?
Are you a storyteller?
Are you an alignment geek?

What Inspires You?

What are your hobbies?
How do you spend your time?
What fascinates you?
This will provide clues to your best themes.

An example: Mary's *Themes*:

Mary's Yoga Branding:	I want to help everyone grow into their most beautiful self.
Mary's passion:	I love to work in my garden.
Mary's strongest *Themes*:	How does our garden grow? The need to weed. Prune the excess, we need light within and without, the first cut yields more growth, etc.
Mary's strongest *HOVs*:	Love, compassion, nurture, cultivate, grow.

Mary tends her garden with love and compassion. She gives the same message to her students with a different, but comfortable *Theme* each week. She does not do as well expressing *HOVs* of power or strength, but she doesn't have to. If she sticks to what she knows, her students will love it.

Chapter Three

Inspiration Takes Perspiration

"The secret to creativity is knowing how to hide your sources."
~ Albert Einstein

Finding inspiration is like finding the key to your car: when you need it, you can't put your finger on it, but you know it's around here somewhere.

I'm not sure I've ever had an original thought. But I'm a great reader, an avid listener, and a voracious student of life. What's more, I always carry a notebook, that way if someone else has an original thought, I can be sure to remember it and make it "mine" sometime soon.

Constructing a theme for a class and finding the inspiration for it happens from the inside out. Many of us frantically search all around for some tidbit or an idea on which to build a class.

I have a friend who teaches yoga in the mountains, and he said to me recently, "I need a new idea. If I theme one more time about the moose, even the moose are going to pack up and move."

The Other Eight Limbed Path

There are eight distinct components to a class theme. I call this the *Other Eight Limbed Path* named after the Yoga Sutras which gave us a path for enlightenment. This path to construct a class will lead straight to your students' hearts, and if you follow it, your themes will find enlightenment too! Your classes will feel fresh and inspired, they will come from your deepest source of authenticity, and they will help to transform your students' lives.

The Other Eight Limbed Path
Eight Steps to Inspired Teaching

1. You: Figure out *who you are*, and *why you teach*. It is the key to finding inspiration.

2. Theme: A phrase, an idiom, a story, an expression. Something easy to remember, and easy to repeat in similar but diverse ways.

3. HOV: The Human Operating Value, or the fundamental quality in each of us that makes us better, wiser and stronger off the mat.

4. Anecdote: A story or narrative that connects the *Theme* to imagery for later reference.

5. Contemplations: Your private thoughts to understand what the *Theme* means to you. Although never seen or heard in public, *Contemplations* have the most reward for your personal growth.

6. Golden Nuggets: Little tidbits and phrases you drop throughout the class. These are the condensed and processed results of your *Contemplations.*

7. WBF: The Why Bother Factor tells your students why they should care about the *Theme.* The *WBF* is often connected to your Yoga Branding. If you can't articulate why the concept is important, it's probably because you don't believe in it yourself, or it isn't aligned with why you teach.

8. Quote: A meaningful phrase which you give to your yogis like a tiny gift. It is the easiest thing to do, but gets the biggest notice from students.

The Eight Steps in Action

The first step on the path starts with "You." In Chapter One, *Understand Your Mission,* we talked about your Yoga Bio, Mission Statement and Yoga Branding, and how it will be the foundation for themes. I can't tell you how many times I have failed in using a great idea, but if it wasn't genuine to me, then it didn't sound right in the room. If it doesn't sound right to you, it won't to anyone else either.

In Chapter Two, *Choose Your Themes Wisely,* we discussed the *Theme* and the *HOV.* The *Theme* is a phrase, an idiom, a story, an expression. It is something easy to remember, or an idea for your class. Students tell me all the time, "Gosh, I love the class you taught about the Honey Badger!" They won't usually say, "I love your class on the meaning of perseverance."

The *HOV* is where you connect your idea to a human emotion that we grapple with in our lives such as fearlessness, strength, perseverance, hope or trust. The *HOV* has meaning, and can put the *Theme* into a person's body and heart. Not all the time, but possibly if you don't connect your *Theme* to an *HOV*, the *Theme* will sound trite or tired. (There are teachers who can teach a stand-alone phrase with meaning, but if you look carefully, there is usually a *HOV* concept lurking beneath it.)

Now let's study the remaining parts of the "Other Eight Limbed Path".

Up to now, I know that some of you have been finding ideas for class by pulling them out of thin air and improvising on your feet. So you might be asking, why do I have to do this much work? Because when you make it up, everyone can tell. The reason we call that stuff cow cookies, or mule muffins, or bull cakes is because you can smell it from a mile away.

MSU is not an Ivy League School

Have you ever been in a class where the teacher seems to effortlessly talk you through a pose and connect to your experience? Where does he get that stuff?

The great teachers find their inspiration everywhere. One of my favorite classes began with a story about how as the instructor was pulling into the parking lot, an older woman took a space out from under his nose. And if that wasn't bad enough, she got out of her car and lectured him about the rule of ladies first. He taught a hilarious class about surrender and gratitude from that one moment.

That instructor was an honorary graduate of 'MSU,' also known as "Make Shit Up" University. Some teachers are simply skilled at making stuff up, and there isn't any subject or idea that they won't make stuff up about. Those of us who think well on our feet are probably familiar with 'MSU.' But 'MSU' is not a terrific school. It is not structured, organized or efficient. The degree you get isn't worth the paper it's written on.

Even if you are able to think spontaneously on your feet and have been theming by the 'MSU' method, it does not create solid classes.

'MSU' is not an Ivy League school.
It is not a reliable system.

On some days you will probably make up some very good stuff, then the next time you go to use it, you've forgotten what you said. Or, and this drives me crazy, you once made up some very good stuff and now you say it all the time like a broken record. Remember, a phrase might be great the first time you say it, and possibly even by the third time. But if you say the same thing over and over, one day you will be committed to a treatment center.

In the end, 'MSU' takes much more time than being organized and it does not produce consistent results. Organization and effort produces results. I know, right? You probably knew this already.

The Eight Steps to Inspiration

A class theme is made up of the following eight parts: *You, Theme, HOV, Anecdotes, Contemplations, Golden Nuggets, Why Bother Factors* (or *WBFs*) and *Quotes. OMG!*

I know some of you just tossed this book and went back to the school of 'MSU.' But hang in there, because this effort will pay off with you teaching better classes, and more freedom in your life to teach a consistently good class in a moment's notice.

The Anecdote

After *You, Theme* and the *HOV*, the next step is the *Anecdote*.

The *Anecdote* is a little story or a narrative or an element of mythology or scripture that sets up your *Theme*. It usually goes in the beginning of a class. Some schools of yoga call the opening minutes of a class the *"dharma"* talk, or a 'centering.' Some styles begin with *pranayama* or breath work and possibly a meditation. I appreciate taking a minute or two before class to focus students because often they are coming from very busy lives and this gives them a chance to settle into the space and put their day aside.

Anecdotes vary tremendously. Some teachers begin their classes by reading from the *Bhagavad Gita* or the *Yoga Sutras* by *Patanjali*. The *Anecdote* could be as simple as a one-liner, or as involved as telling a mythological tale about the Hindu Deity Ganesha. Some teachers might lead with a quote from B.K.S. Iyengar, or from a really outstanding yoga memoir that is organized into chapters based on the *Themes* she used in the classroom (shameless plug for my first book, *Finding More on the Mat: How I Grew Better, Wiser and Stronger through Yoga.*).

It is entirely up to you on how you want to begin your class. In fact, you do not have to use an *Anecdote* to start the class! You can begin with *Pranayama* or three *Oms*, and then tell the *Anecdote* in the early sequences to foreshadow the *Theme*. You want to use an *Anecdote* early so you can refer back to it during the body of the class. If you tell your *Anecdote* at the end of class, students will have less of an idea how that related to the yoga they just experienced. Furthermore, you lost an opportunity to connect visual imagery to the idea in your class.

Effective *Anecdotes* are told quickly, succinctly, and provide enough clarity to state the *Theme*. Furthermore, they should be interesting enough that you can refer back to their imagery as a verbal reminder of the *Theme* during *asana* instruction.

Do you have to use an *Anecdote*? Not really. However, it becomes mind-numbingly dull to open your class everyday with "Today's *Theme* is 'Love.'" Or, "Today's *Theme* is be kind to unicorns." Or, "Today's *Theme* is surrender." If you are not interesting, you will be ignored.

Anecdote attributes:

Every *Anecdote* is different, but each one must:
- Be succinct.
- Be universalized.
- Connect to yoga.
- Connect to life off the mat.

Be clear. Be succinct. Make every word tell.

Most yoga teachers could use a big cup of shut up, and never more so than in the beginning of class. There must be something about finally being the focus of everyone's attention and so now we are going to milk it for all it's worth. This is so middle child syndrome. We can have all the time in the world and all the therapy money can buy to work out our need for attention, but the first few minutes of yoga class is not the place.

The more your *Anecdote* is clear and succinct, the more your students will give you their full attention. If you tend to wander, so will their attention. If you have trouble keeping yourself to three minutes, they will start their practice while you are talking. If you have trouble making your point, they will not know what you are talking about for the rest of the class. If you aren't sure if you are taking too long, look at your watch, or look at your students. They will tell you what you need to know if they are yawning. Once I was going on and on and a yogi actually started doing push-ups! Note to self: shut up!

If you run out of time and the students are getting restless, you can always elaborate on your *Anecdote* during the class. I often tell my *Anecdote* in a minute (maybe a football minute), and then elaborate little bits of the story during the warm up moves. Whatever it is you want to say, you can weave it into the class so your students can begin to practice. Remember, they came for yoga.

Universalize the Anecdote

The next step to the *Anecdote* is to universalize it. It is important to connect the story to your students so it does not appear to be all about you! A great universalizing moment also involves your students in the class and gives them some skin in the game. There is nothing worse than having a teacher go on and on about their life and you are thinking: Hello? Is there anybody else in this room? Do you even know we are here? Really, trust me; *nobody wants to hear about you.* But they do want to hear about them.

Universalize your *Anecdote* and draw them into your story with one of the following statements, or something similar:

Universalizing statements:

- Has this ever happened to you?
- Did you ever feel this way?
- Can you relate?
- Do you know someone like this?
- I hope I'm not alone here...
- Do you know what I'm talking about?
  And P.S., wait for the heads to nod before you move on.

Only Connect

Once you stated your *Anecdote,* and you asked the students if this ever happened to them, it's important to connect it to the *Theme,* to yoga and finally to how it might relate to life off the mat. This sounds complicated, but if you thought your *Anecdote* was a good story, then you probably know how it relates to yoga.

Connecting the *Anecdote*:

Try something similar to the following phrases:

- "This story is just like yoga in that we have to FILL IN THE BLANK."
- "Yoga is just like life in that we FILL IN THE BLANK."

Connecting the *Anecdote* to yoga might seem ridiculously obvious, especially since you are teaching a yoga class and not riding the subway or something, but I can't tell you how many students will have no idea how it relates unless you tell them. Our job is to make their path just a little easier, and being clear always helps.

Awesome Anecdotes

One of the very best *Anecdotes* I ever heard came from a teacher who was getting married. He started class with this:

> *"My fiancé and I were talking, and she asked me to promise that we would be together always. I told her, there are no guarantees! In the case of love, none are necessary, and in the case of fear, none are strong enough."*

In just one minute, this teacher set up a lovely class on the *HOVs* of "love" and "fear," and how to trust your way through uncertainty. This was so much more memorable than if he started the class by saying, "Today we are going to talk about fear."

More Anecdote Examples:

- "The yoga sutras begin with *"Atha."* Atha means now. Now we begin the practice of yoga. Not later, now."

- "I was watching "Good Morning America" and saw they hired a talent scout to turn an ordinary person on the street into a super model. So I got to thinking, what if each of us had a super model inside us waiting to shine?"

- "There is a story in Hindu mythology about Lakshmi and how this goddess of beauty had a stain on her dress. She had to wear it to a wedding, so she decided to dye her dress a vibrant red color. In this way, she made her problem her symbol of beauty."

- "Driving home yesterday I was stuck in traffic when I saw a sign that said, "If you lived here, you'd be home now." And I realized what if I had already arrived?"

The Last Most Important Thing about Anecdotes

However you choose to start your class, there is one important rule:

Five Minutes to the Move
No Exceptions. Ever.*

---

*So, I will make an exception, of course. If you have been teaching for years and have a steady following, and everyone likes to hear you talk for 25 minutes before class, by all means continue. Who am I to tell you to change your style? Also, workshops that last for more than two hours can have a longer opening or *dharma* talk.

But please, don't work so hard to find exceptions to this rule. Work harder to follow this rule, and you will have students who pay attention to what you have to say.

A criticism of yoga teachers throughout the world is there is too much talk. Honestly, when yoga was created it was about breath and movement. Not even in the *Yoga Sutras* does it say it's about talk. It has always been about shutting up! We need more time to focus our minds and expand our breath, and less time talking.

Five minutes to the move means, five minutes to complete the welcoming, the *Anecdote,* breath work and meditation. Then everyone needs to be on their feet practicing *asana.* Presumably, that's why they came.

Contemplation

Great classes need great *Contemplation.* Once you have an idea for a *Theme,* there is only one way to make it inspiring: think about it. This is the part that takes time. But it also has the biggest payoff. When I take the time to study about my idea, I feel more confident in the room and the students can tell which gives them more trust in the teachings.

Contemplation is where many of us fall short in class preparation because it requires time and focused effort. You cannot wing it. Remember 'MSU?' Making stuff up does not always work. It is hard to come up with those revealing and life-changing insights for your students unless you've thought about it.

Contemplations are your thoughts about the theme. Write your observations in your journal, on the back of an envelope, on the back of a piece of paper or on a computer. You can be speaking with a friend and come up with something awesome, and then write it down quickly in a notebook. Sometimes I ask my phone to take a memo while I'm driving. However you do it, be sure to save that thought for later. Saving it, re-using it, and digesting it elevates this stuff from the school of 'MSU' into something concrete.

Interestingly, your *Contemplations* may never see the light of day. They are the rough, diary form of your thoughts. Nobody may ever see them. They are private. *Contemplation* is used for the most important part of your journey as a yoga teacher: self-discovery.

But while the *Contemplations* never see the light of day, they form the basis for the public part of your teaching, the *Golden Nuggets*. It is the *Golden Nuggets* that make your class memorable and motivating.

Golden Nuggets

The *Golden Nuggets* are the digested, considered, condensed and most awesome part of your *Contemplations*. They are the brilliant insights you came up with from the rough drafts. But most of all, they are brief, concise moments of clarity.

For example: let's say you have spent some time contemplating a pose, such as Handstand. You may have kept a yoga diary of all your attempts, your failures, your insights, your achievements and your overwhelming feelings of suckiness (I might be projecting here). It is not a good idea to regurgitate this mess of low self-esteem on your students. They will have their own yoga messes to deal with on the mat.

However, after a lifetime of working a pose, perhaps you've learned something? If you can condense this wisdom, you can create a *Golden Nugget.*

After all my whining, self-pity, and brief moments of exuberance only to be followed by a devastating fall, here are the *Golden Nuggets* I use to teach Handstand:

Golden Nuggets for Handstand

- There are no overnight success stories.
- No effort is ever wasted.
- Sometimes the pose is already in us, and we need to trust it.
- It's not about the pose; it's what you can learn from it.

Golden Nuggets are used as inspiration throughout a class. When you are moving your students from pose to pose, dropping a *Golden Nugget* is like sprinkling fairy dust on the room. Instant magic happens. If a student cannot grasp what it means to "spiral her thigh," she might at least understand that her effort is not wasted. And suddenly, she feels better. *Golden Nuggets* connect the power of inspiration to motivation on the mat.

Favorite Golden Nuggets from the Nugget Masters:

- Yoga is like the Lottery. You must be present to win. (Darren Rhodes)
- You have to shape shift, to state shift. (Darren Rhodes)
- Remember the light. (Christina Sell)
- You want to be ready when the expansion comes. (Chris Muchow)
- If you want to be here, you have to show up. (Baron Baptiste)
- Find your inner badass. (Amy Ippoliti)

One word of warning: A little nugget goes a long way. *Golden Nuggets* are heavy duty moments of inspiration and you do not want to take too much away from the *asana*. You only want to enhance the *asana*, so go easy in your class.

Golden Nuggets are like spices in a stew.
If you use too many, or mix them up, the stew is a mess.

Stay on track, stay with your *Theme* and you will be a success. If your *Theme* is about surrender, don't suddenly bring in: "Must be present to win." It makes no sense. Remember the warning about switching horses? I am waving my arms wildly here to remind you to not, DO NOT, ever switch or mix up your *Themes* and *HOVs* or drop indiscriminate *Golden Nuggets*. It drives students crazy.

Lastly, you will probably prepare many more *Golden Nuggets* than you will actually use in a class. For a 60 to 90 minute class, you only need three to five nuggets. There are times you want to move your students from pose to pose, and times you want them to pause and reflect. Do not drop a *Golden Nugget* with every pose. That would be a distraction to the yoga.

Lastly, the *asana* and breath are more important than every little thing you thought to say. Be mindful of the student's practice of all aspects of yoga, including *asana* and inspiration, and you will be a 'Theme Weaver', not a 'Theme Deceiver!'

The Why Bother Factor

The Why Bother Factor, or the *WBF*, is where you tie your *Theme* to the reason why you teach. This is the moment of truth. I call it the "smell test." If you can't clearly state why your students should believe your *Theme*, then perhaps you don't believe it yourself? This is a moment of clarity where you can be honest about why you chose the *Theme*. If you can't say it, you may not believe it, and your students won't buy it at all.

Fundamentally, the *WBF* is the "because" factor. Why does any of this matter? Why should your students listen to your themes? Why should they surrender anything at all? Why should they show up for your class? Because...

For example, I have heard many times that I should "just let go." Why? Frankly, I like being an uptight New Yorker, and the more you tell me to "let go," the more I am going to fight it. But if the teacher gave me a good reason, such as, "If you let go of your anger, then your teenagers will see you being peaceful and everyone will stop fighting in your house," then it might make me stop and think; maybe there is something to this yoga stuff?

You must believe in your *Themes* or your students won't believe them either. They will tune you out. I also feel this way with the harder poses. If the teacher asks me to do some crazy pose, and does not give me a good reason on why I should bother, I will probably sit it out. But if you say, "Try this pose because finding balance on the mat will help you find balance off the mat," then I will be more inclined to try. I have a reason to do it.

Ways to WBF your theme:

To state the *WBF* and make the *Theme* meaningful for your students, follow this simple "IF...Then" formula:

"If everyone was able to <u>STATE THE *THEME*</u>, then <u>THIS WOULD BE ACCOMPLISHED</u>.

Or this variation:

> "When you STATE THE *THEME*,
> then THIS WOULD BE ACCOMPLISHED.

Ultimately, the WBF is tied to your Yoga Brand

OMG, I knew I should have done that Yoga Branding thing! Right? Well it's not too late. The *WBF* is the ultimate smell test for your yoga branding.

Yoga Branding We Loved

Here are some of the Yoga Brands from Chapter One, *Understand Your Mission*, which we will use to create a *Why Bother Factor* statement for our yoga classes. If these seem hard to say, it could be because they are not your yoga brands. That's why I call the *WBF* the "smell" test. If you can't say it, you probably don't believe it. But someone else can rock these brands wonderfully, as you will soon rock your own.

A Few of the Yoga Brands:

- Feel worthy of greatness.
- Heal physically and spiritually.
- Connect to a larger purpose.
- Find peace in our busy lives.
- Feel accepted and good enough as we are.

Tied to a WBF:

- "Because something happened here, we feel more worthy with every pose."

- "If we practiced with compassion, the hurts and injuries in our lives would start to heal."

- "When you connect with community, then you will feel support from your friends."

- "If everyone was able to let go of the noise in their life, then they'd have more peaceful energy for the people they love."

- "If you recognized your inner beauty, then you would know you are good enough just as you are."

WBF your theme with your Yoga Brand:

To state the *WBF* with your *Yoga Brand*, follow this formula:

"If everyone was able to <u>STATE THE *THEME*</u>, then <u>YOUR YOGA BRAND WOULD BE ACCOMPLISHED</u>.

The *Why Bother Factor* then becomes a very powerful part of the class because you will state your idea in the unique format of your brand. No other teacher on the planet will believe in your *Theme* exactly as you do. Therefore, this is the single, most distinctive moment of your class. It is your signature, if you will. It is your yoga moment to shine and to bring a hit of enlightenment to your students.

However, because it is so very powerful you do not need to do it more than once, or at the very most just twice in a class.

— DO NOT —
Drop a WBF every time you drop a Golden Nugget.
Once is enough.

The students do not need to hear how they can change the world every time they take a breath. That's a lot of pressure! Likewise, you do not need constantly to tell someone, "Just let go or else your children are going to end up in therapy." They probably already know it anyway. It's powerful, and it belongs just once or twice in a class and near the end of your session.

Lastly, the *WBF* is often the hardest part of the eight steps for teachers to comprehend and execute. Whenever I coach teachers in workshops, this is the part they stumble on.

Consider this: The *WBF* is not completely necessary in teaching a *Theme*. In fact, teaching a *Theme* is not entirely necessary for teaching yoga. If you do not state the *WBF*, the world is not going to end. However, if you cannot state why your students should believe your *Theme*, then perhaps you do not believe it yourself?

However, this is also true: If you do not state the *WBF*, *then you pass on the single most distinctive moment of your class.* It is your yoga moment to shine and to bring a hit of enlightenment to your students, so if you pass on it, you pass on the moment to define yourself as a teacher, just saying.

Quotes

After all the work you do to build your class, the easiest part is often the thing students love the most. That would be the *Quote*.

A *Quote* is most effectively used at the end or in the beginning of class. Sometimes I like to use a *Quote* at the beginning of class as my *Anecdote,* or at the end as a gift to the students. That way, your students will actually remember it. If I used it in the middle, it feels like I just tossed it out there without a proper staging or introduction.

These days you can easily find *Quotes* on the Internet. I recommend Brainy Quote, Quote Garden and ThinkExist websites, but there are many others as well. There are sites dedicated to the quotes of Rumi, B.K.S. Iyengar and Patanjali. You can also read a book!

One warning about using a *Quote*: If you drop an overused, clichéd quote by Rumi, then you must support it. If you do not support it with a *Theme,* an *HOV, Anecdotes* and *Golden Nuggets,* then you have committed a real yoga faux pas. This is lazy teaching and someone may hang themselves (me).

Using a *Quote* at the end of class is the finishing touch. It is a like a thoughtful gift you found for your students. Interestingly, the *Quote* often takes the least amount of time to find as compared to the time spent doing *Contemplations,* but yields the most praise from our students. Go figure.

I know of a teacher who printed the *Quote* onto pieces of paper and then folded them into an origami. At the end of class, she placed one on each student's mat. When they arose from *Savasana,* they had their tiny quote as a gift to take home. Her class became a not-to-be-missed event! If someone had to miss, they would call her and ask if she could please save them an origami. That's how to build a following with your class preparation.

In Summary

Classes start with a seed of an idea and then take work. Even those of us who are good at thinking on our feet are probably working much harder than those of us who get organized ahead of time. The good news, however, is that once you do the work, you will probably be able to use your efforts over and over again. The school of 'MSU' is not efficient. But becoming a 'Theme Weaver' is very efficient. If it takes you an hour per class the first few times you do it, it will start to take just a few minutes as you get more skilled. What's more, you will pack a wallop of inspiration and motivation for your students each time you take your seat at the front of the room.

SAMPLE TIMINGS

The Opening: Five Minutes to the Move!

Welcome your students. The opening might include *pranayama*, meditation or a centering. Taking this time helps your students focus on their practice and leave the world behind. The general rule is five minutes to the move in a regular class. The students come to yoga for yoga, and not for talk.

Ideal for: The *Anecdote,* or *Quote,* and/or state the *Theme*

****

The Body of the Class

The body of the class is the *asana* or posture sequence. Good times for inspiration are during the second side of a pose after you explained the alignment, a demonstration, when explaining a prop, or if there is a moment when you have the students' attention.

Ideal for: Three to Five *Golden Nuggets,* Possibly the *WBF*

****

The Cool Down

Toward the end of class, when students are unwinding is an excellent time to reaffirm the theme. This could be a good opportunity for the *Why Bother Factor* as well.

Ideal for: *Quote* or *WBF*

****

The Closing

At the end of class, you may have an option to leave your students in meditation, but it is also an excellent time to emphasize your *Theme*. Ending the class with something strong such as your *Quote* or *Anecdote* creates a memorable experience. You might also state the *WBF* if you haven't done so yet. Remember the teacher who made an origami for her students with a quote inside? This is your last chance to leave them with something special, so take your time and wish them well.

Ideal for: *Quote* or *WBF,* or restate the *Theme*

Chapter Four

Simple Themes to Spin Dreams

"If you can't help them, at least don't hurt them."
~ Dalai Lama

If you just turned to this page in the book, it will be a lot like jumping into an intermediate yoga class before learning the foundations. Can you do it? Yes, of course. Will you get as much out of it? Probably not.

So, hopefully you have done the work. You have your Yoga Bio, Mission Statement and Yoga Branding. You know the concepts that speak to you, and you know the difference between a *Theme* and a *Human Operating Value* (*HOV*). Lastly, you know how to support your idea with *Anecdotes, Contemplations, Golden Nuggets,* the *Why Bother Factor* and *Quotes.*

Now let's create some great themes.

What's a Great Theme?

A great theme has one purpose:

A great theme transforms lives.

What is important about a theme is not how complicated it is. It doesn't matter if you quote Buddha or Bon Jovi or the *Bhagavad Gita*. This is the only thing that makes a theme great:

It only matters if it matters,
First to you, and then to your students.

A great theme is one that:
- Speaks to you.
- Resonates after the class.
- Has the potential to motivate on the mat.
- Has the potential to motivate off the mat.
- Is able to reveal more about the self.
- Creates an expansion of who we are.
- Illuminates something either about us, about yoga, or about the world.
- Is motivating, inspiring, and enlightening.
- Is all of the above, or just one of the above.

What is not a great theme?
- Any theme that does not speak to you. Your students will know, and they won't buy it either.
- Any theme that does not speak to your audience. For example, talking incessantly about kids to a room of young dudes (note to self).
- A theme that is too specific. For example, your kitchen renovation. We don't care, unless you universalize it.

- A theme that is too general. Beware of clichés such as "Just let go." Relate the theme to something meaningful, i.e., let go of fear and find courage.
- You. In general, you are not that interesting. Not you, not your marriage, or your non-marriage, or your kids, or God forbid, your sick cat. You are only interesting in that you relate your revelations to your class so it be comes about them.

The *One Word Theme*: Sweet and Simple

The most straightfoward, versatile and basic approach is the *One Word Theme*.

The *One Word Theme* is sweet, concise, and powerful when done right. It packs a wallop of enlightenment with minimal wordiness. Everyone can understand it. And, in general, you won't get lost teaching it.

One of the most adroit users of the one word theme is Darren Rhodes, an internationally known yoga teacher and Director of YogaOasis in Tucson, Arizona. Darren's teaching is like his *asana* practice (he is the model for the book, *Yoga Resource*, demonstrating 400 yoga poses in perfect pitch): He is studied, practiced, subtle and refined.

Darren appreciates the *One Word Theme* as it is beautiful, and simple. It gives you a chance to explore the word and its connections and synonyms, so that it becomes meaningful to your students.

Some excellent word choices:

- Arrive
- Dedicate
- Expand
- Listen
- Enjoy
- Integrate
- Align
- Connect
- Believe
- Pause

The *HOV* as the *Theme*

You may notice that choosing a *One Word Theme* is a lot like identifying your *Human Operating Value*, or *HOV* for your *Theme*. Remember to choose a word that is in alignment with your Mission Statement, or else it won't be authentic. Even though the approach seems straightforward, if you choose badly you will have a struggle to communicate.

Many years ago, I received some excellent advice from my mentor when I first started teaching yoga. I didn't know what music to play in the class, if any. She advised me that it really didn't matter if I played music as long as I liked either the songs or the silence. If I'm having a good time, so will my students. The same is exactly true with your *Theme* and *HOV* choice. If you enjoy it, so will they.

The benefit of using a *One Word Theme* or using your *HOV* for a *Theme* is that it's simple, clean and direct. But you must still do the work. You must find the *Anecdotes, Golden Nuggets,* the *WBF* and *Quotes* so that you are not saying your word over and over again like a broken record.

Sample Theme: Arrive!

Let's begin by choosing a word that can mean many things to many people. "Arrive" is a versatile word. It can be interpreted as to feel a sense of peace and contentment with where you are at this moment. It can be understood to be that you have arrived in your life with accomplishment and expertise. Or it can also mean that you are completely present. Those are three different *HOVs* with the word "Arrive."

Let's create a sample theme on "Arrive." For this sample, I will use an *HOV* of presence.

Arrive!

You:	Your Yoga Branding. What is your intention in teaching?
Theme:	"Arrive"
HOVs:	Be present, awake, aware
Anecdote:	On the way to work today I saw a sign that said, "If you lived here, you would be home now." I realized that instead of being stuck in traffic, or coming and going, I could be here, now. I would have arrived!

Contemplations: I often feel that I'm exhausted with the "journey," and I just want to feel like I got somewhere with my practice and my life. If I was present, I'd already be home. We are where we are supposed to be. Wherever I roll out my mat, I feel present and at home. If I wasn't so busy, I'd have more time! If I wasn't commuting, I'd be here. My life feels like I am always commuting and reaching for something else. Maybe I have what I need?

Golden Nuggets:
- The journey might be overrated!
- My mat is home.
- We are where we are supposed to be.
- Stop commuting. You have arrived.
- Welcome yourself home. Arrive.
- Awake to *this* moment.
- If you weren't so busy, you'd be present.
- Be here now.
- Life isn't later. It is now.

WBF: When you realize you are exactly where you are supposed to be, you have "arrived." If you stop commuting, then you will find

> more value in the present moment and be more present for the ones you love. Life doesn't happen later. It is now. (I used my Yoga Brand, which is "finding more out of life." You could easily state this with any other reason to practice yoga, such as healing.)

Quote: "We shall not cease from exploration, and the end of all our exploring will be to arrive where we started and know the place for the first time." – T.S. Eliot

"Be here now." – Ram Dass

Teach Here Now!

To teach this *Theme*, remember how it might look in the room from Chapter Three, *Inspiration Takes Perspiration*, which demonstrated sample timings. While you are becoming more comfortable with pacing, try to remember that your yoga sequence and the breath should always be the focus, and the inspiration you use is like magic fairy dust you sprinkle on the class to motivate the students.

The goal is to intertwine inspiration without becoming a distraction from the yoga. Less is more! We want to add depth without disruption. The best instructors still let the *asana* take center stage.

Now let's look at how we might express this theme in a typical class.

The Opening: Anecdote or Quote:

On the way to work today I saw a sign that said, "If you lived here, you would be home now." I realized that I often feel like I'm running from here to there in a constant commute. Do you feel like this, where you are always on the move? (Wait for heads to nod). I wonder if instead of commuting to somewhere else, let's practice being exactly where we are supposed to be. Let's trust that we have 'Arrived!'"

Then you either shut up, or "Om," or lead them in *Pranayama*. But remember:

Five minutes to the move.
No exceptions. Ever!

The Body of the Class: Golden Nuggets and possibly the WBF

The warm up phase of the class is an excellent time to elaborate on the *Anecdote* if you didn't get a chance to fully explain your intention in the opening. It is very important to be brief in the beginning, and respect the students' expectation of practicing yoga and not experiencing a lecture on yoga philosophy. That includes reciting every Yoga Sutra on the value of presence (including the whole point of practice) and the last lecture from your Tantra teacher. However, if you wish to mention these things, then by all means do so during the warm up.

In this case, I did not get a chance to relate the *Anecdote* to yoga, which is a big no-no. There will always be a student in the room who does not know why I am talking about driving in a yoga class. So for her, I might say, "I got to thinking that my commute is just like yoga, in that I am always looking for the next big thing and I don't realize when I actually have a pose. What if I have already 'arrived' at my best pose? What if being present in this moment, is the best pose of all?"

The main body of the class, after the warm up and before the cool down, is where you drop your *Golden Nuggets*. Remember, you should have more *Golden Nuggets* than you will actually use. You only need three to five per class to drop one every 10 minutes or so. A good one to use might be, "Perhaps we are where we are supposed to be."

Continue to drop your nuggets during the body of the class. Ideal times would be whenever there is a pause in the action. If you are asking the students to hold a pose or to watch a demonstration, these are perfect opportunities to drop a little nugget. Remember, you only need three to five opportunities over an hour class, or one approximately every 15 minutes. You are not dropping a nugget every time your students come up for air. Furthermore, you may not use all your *Golden Nuggets* in one class, but they are good to know just in case one works better than another depending on how the class evolved.

Golden Nugget Opportunities:

- The Warm Up
- Demos
- Peak poses
- Partnering moments
- Introducing props
- Breaks in the action

- The second side of a pose, if you cued alignment on the first
- When you want to explain the intention behind a pose

The Cool Down—WBF or possibly the Quote

After the main body of the class and an apex pose (if you use one), most styles of yoga will incorporate a cool down phase where the students relax, twist and prepare for meditation or *savasana*. Because you have their attention, and because they are beginning to relax, this is an excellent time to use your *Quote* or the *WBF, Why Bother Factor*. The *WBF* might sound like this: "When you realize you are exactly where you are supposed to be, you stop commuting and you arrive. Then you will find value in the here and now, and be more present for the ones you love." Shazam!

The Closing—Ideal for Quote, possibly WBF

The *Quote* is the delicious cherry on top for your class. Remember the teacher who wrapped up her *Quote* in an origami piece? The *Quote* is a gift for your students. It gives students something to think about. Remember to pause after you say it so the students can take it in.

For this class, let's use: "We shall not cease from exploration, and the end of all our exploring will be to arrive where we started and know the place for the first time." T.S. Eliot. Then I might add, "I wish you happy travels, but most of all, I wish that you know when you have arrived." Or I might say, "Life isn't later. It is now." And end with, "Namaste."

The *One Word Theme* is not "E-A-S-Y."

The *One Word Theme* on the surface appears simple. But underneath every great *Theme*, whether it is based on one word or the *Yoga Sutras*, there is a mountain of work supporting it. And even though it is just one W-O-R-D, it is still easy to get L-O-S-T.

Getting lost is easy. For example, you planned a class on "presence" and by the end of class you were talking about "contentment." Whoa baby, you started in Kansas but you ended up in Oz.

Preparation goes a long way to preventing mishaps in the room, even with the *One Word Theme*. If you prepare, you will have a better chance at creating a class that packs a wallop of motivation and enlightenment for your students.

Pros and Cons

Pros of using a *One Word Theme*:
Clear, concise, direct and effective. Enables a strong connection with practice. The *HOV* is usually clearly understood, if not the actual *Theme*.

Cons of using a *One Word Theme*:
At risk for repetition and over-simplifying life.

Adding a *Theme* to Your *HOV*

Using a *One Word Theme* based on a *HOV* is an excellent approach to connecting inspiration to perspiration for your classes. It is highly effective and not terribly intrusive to the practice of yoga.

It is especially well-suited for new yoga teachers who are also learning to juggle many balls in the air: the room environment, the sequence, the pace, alignment cues, the complainer and the student who is standing on their head. And don't forget to make sure the students are safe! Sometimes it is more than enough to use a *One Word Theme*.

However, if you feel you are ready for more, then you might try the next step. If a *One Word Theme* is typically using a *HOV* as a stand-alone theme, then the next step would be to combine a phrase or an idiom with your *HOV*. This would be to use a *Theme* with your *HOV*.

The main advantage to adding a *Theme* into the mix is flexibility. Creating a *Theme* to use with an *HOV* gives you more opportunity to re-use the *One Word Themes* you created with minimal repetition. Less work, more glory, 'nuff said.

Another advantage to adding a phrase or an idiom to your *HOV*, is you also create more versatility in the images available to convey your idea. You become a storyteller for your students. These stories and images create a lasting impression. Students are more likely to remember a *Theme*, than a word. For example, students tell me all the time, "I love your class on the Honey Badger." They do not say, "I love your class on perseverance." Or they might say, "I loved the story of the boy on Colfax". They do not say, "I need to find hope in my life."

Sample Theme: *Atha*

Let's create another *Theme*. For this example, I will use the phrase, "*Atha* – Now begins the study of yoga," which is the first Yoga Sutra from Patanjali. And I will use the *HOV* of "contentment."

"*Atha* – Now Begins the Study of Yoga."

You: Your Yoga Branding. What is your intention in teaching?

Theme: "*Atha* – Now begins the study of yoga."

HOVs: Compassion, contentment and ease

Anecdote: On the way to work today I saw a sign that said, "If you lived here, you would be home." It made me think of the first yoga sutra, "Atha, now begins the study of yoga." I realized that instead of always looking for more in my life, I could be happy and content right now! Yoga begins now; not in the future when you think you are going to be perfect, but when we are content with what we have.

Contemplations: Yoga doesn't begin when you are ready to find the time to get on your mat. Yoga begins not when it is easy, but when it is hard. It doesn't begin when you want to be more flexible or stronger, or when you want to get out of a pose, or when you lose 10 pounds, or when you want to quit. *Atha* is now,

not later. Contentment is now.
There is no journey, there is only now.
Now means we take the good with the
bad. Now we get off the bus or the
commute and be at home. Now we
reach our destination. Now we are
a yogi. Come as you are, because you
are ready now.

Golden Nuggets:
- *Atha!* Now begins the study of yoga.
- Contentment is now. Come as you are to your mat.
- Yoga is when you have compassion for your hamstrings.
- Welcome yourself home by being happy with where you are.
- Arrive at your practice. Not your perfect.
- With each breath, arrive at contentment.
- Recognize that you are complete.

WBF:
If yoga begins now, then you have arrived. Even if you bring an extra 10 pounds, or a bad hair day, or a sense that you want more, if yoga begins now, then you are here. Radiating this attitude makes everyone around you feel better with what they have too. Stop the commute. You are home.

Quotes:	"*Atha* – Now begins the study of yoga." – Patanjali "Rather than have what you want, can you want what you have?" – Proverb

Sample Theme: *Atha* with Surrender

By adding the *Theme* of "*Atha* – Now Begins the Study of Yoga," to our original class on "Arrive," we have two classes. Furthermore, looking at our new class, it reads very differently than the original class on "Arrive." The first class focused primarily on "presence." The second focused on "contentment." In this way, we created two very distinct classes, but we were able to reuse some of the *Golden Nuggets* and *Contemplations* from the first class. This enabled us to save time and re-use valuable inspiration.

Now let's use the *Theme* of "*Atha* – Now Begins the Study of Yoga" with the *HOV* of "surrender" to see a completely new way of reusing this *Theme*.

"*Atha* – Now Begins the Study of Yoga."

You:	Your Unique Yoga Branding. What is your intention in teaching?
Theme:	"*Atha* – Now begins the study of yoga."
HOV:	Surrender, Acceptance, Compassion.

Anecdote:	I was in the line at Starbucks when the barista messed up my order. I wanted to scream. But instead I said, "That's okay. Can I help?" Patanjali tells us that yoga begins now, "*Atha.*" Yoga doesn't begin when you are in your happy place. Yoga begins when the barista messes up your order. When you want to scream and you say, "Thank you" instead, that is yoga.
Contemplations:	Surrender may look like "Thank you." Surrender is not always being right. Surrender means the other person could be right. It could be shutting up when you want to scream. Surrender is not later when you've had a chance to calm down. Surrender is now. Surrender is being patient in traffic. Surrender is realizing you live here, not somewhere else, in this moment. This is your home. Arrive at surrender.
Golden Nuggets:	• *Atha* – Now begins the study of yoga. • Now begins in Handstand, not in *Savasana*! • Now you practice yoga, when you want to scream.

	• "Thank you," not "f-you."
	• Surrender begins when your order is messed up.
	• Surrender may look like shutting up.
WBF:	"If everyone knew that surrender looks like forgiveness, then Starbucks would be a happier place. And the roads would be safer! And we would find more ease in our life."
Quotes:	"*Atha* – Now begins the study of yoga." – Patanjali "Thank you is the new F-You." – Michelle Berman Marchildon

"Now!" (sorry, I couldn't resist) we have three distinct classes from the same tiny seed of inspiration. The first class was "Arrive," and focused on presence. The second class included a *Theme* of "Atha – Now Begins the Study of Yoga," and changed the focus to "contentment." The third class kept the *Theme* of "Atha," but changed the *HOV* to "surrender." In each case we were able to reuse bits and pieces of our previous classes, but yet created a very new experience for our students.

Thus, the main advantage of using both a *Theme* and an *HOV* is that now instead of having one class on the word "Arrive," you have created three. Truly, though, the possibilities are endless when you mix and match a *Theme* and an *HOV*.

Pros and Cons

Pros of using a *One Word Theme*:
Still direct and effective as with a *One Word Theme*, but now it gives the student a story or a phrase to remember the practice. You also have new *Contemplations* and *Golden Nuggets* which you can reuse in the future.

Cons of using a *One Word Theme* and an *HOV*:
Harder to prepare than using a *One Word Theme*. Easier to get lost and switch *HOVs* by accident in the middle of a class. Also still at risk for over simplifying life.

"All the great things are simple,
And many can be expressed in a single word:
Freedom, justice, honor, duty, mercy, hope."
Winston Churchill

The Other Eight Limbed Path Standard Format

You: Write your Yoga Branding at the top of every "Theme Sheet". It is the key to stating the *Why Bother Factor*. It also helps remind you why you teach before you step into the room.

Theme: If you are using a unique concept, then write down a phrase, an idiom, a figure of speech, or an expression. Make it something easy to remember.

HOV: Write down your *Human Operating Value*. It is the fundamental quality that is transformational underlying the meaning of the class. Create one or two synonyms so you don't sound like a broken record.

Anecdote: Write and practice a story or phrase or narrative that sets the tone and provides imagery for the class. It must be succinct, universalized and related to yoga and life. It must be completed in time to honor the rule, "Five Minutes to the Move."

Contemplate: Journal privately to understand what the theme means to you. Although not spoken out loud, *Contemplations* have the most reward for your teaching and personal growth.

Golden Nuggets: Tidbits and phrases you create from your *Contemplations* which you drop throughout the class. These lend inspiration and motivation to the theme. Create five to six, of which you will use three to five for a standard class.

You may not use them all, but they are good to have in your back pocket.

WBF: The *Why Bother Factor* tells students why they should care and practice yoga. It connects the *Theme* to your Yoga Branding, and makes it a unique experience from every other teacher's offering. Nobody will have the same *Theme* and the same reasons to practice as you. NOBODY. This is often the hardest step to articulate, but also the most rewarding for your students.

Quote: The *Quote* is the cherry on top. Use it at the beginning, or the end, but be sure to pause after saying it so the students can take it in. Either find a *Quote,* or use a strong mnemonic phrase they can remember and take with them off the mat.

Chapter Five

Working the Multi-Part Theme

When I stand before God at the end of my life,
I would hope that I would not have a single bit of talent left,
And could say, 'I used everything you gave me'."
~ Erma Bombeck

Confucius said, "Life is really simple, but we insist on making it complicated."

Of course we do.

The model in Chapter Four, *Simple Themes to Spin the Dreams*, which explains the *One Word Theme* based on a *Human Operating Value* is a very good model. There is no reason you have to read any further in this book. The *One Word Theme* can carry you to becoming a Yoga Celebrity. You can (and probably should because it is clear and concise) record videos and teach at yoga festivals with a *One Word Theme*. But most importantly, it can transform your students for the better.

Nevertheless, just in case you want to try your hand at a little more, then here it is. But don't say you haven't been warned. It gets complicated; remember to breathe.

The *Twofold Theme*

The *Twofold Theme*, or one that recognizes there are two sides to every story and to every *Human Operating Value,* can provide a richer experience for your students. By creating a dual outlook, it allows your students to identify with the part that speaks to them the most that day. For example, someone may need a boost to try something new in their lives, while another may need a shot of self-acceptance that she is good enough just as she is at that moment.

A drawback to the *One Word Theme*, or even to a *Theme* combined with an *HOV*, is that it tends to over simplify the world for your students. You can tell them to "Arrive," but what if they are not in a place where they can hear the message? I cannot tell you how many times I have been working hard to finish a book or complete a project, and a yoga teacher tells me to "Just let go." Really? Should I throw it out? Should I give up because life got a little busy? Should Michelangelo have quit when he got to the part of the Sistine Chapel when the ladder was a little short? On those days I probably needed to hear, "Hang on tight."

My kids understand this too. Whenever they want to watch TV instead of doing their homework, they tell me, "Mom, we are just trying to be good yogis and let this homework stuff go." I can hear my mother laughing that I am getting what I deserve: smart-mouthed kids.

A *Twofold Theme* is a more sophisticated in its worldview than taking just a one-sided perspective. And you have a greater chance of casting a wider net for supporting more of your students.

For example, let's take "Arrive." I use a variation of this theme whenever I need to reaffirm self-acceptance. Plus, it's really fun to say, "Look to the top of your mat, jump and arrive!" But for the sake of argument, let's see what happens when we try to make this theme more balanced for the students who may need another type of motivation.

Contemplate for the *Twofold Theme*

The first step to contemplate for the *Twofold Theme* is to consider both sides of the story.

What happens when you "Arrive?"

- You recognize you are where you are supposed to be.
- You feel self-worth.
- You are content.

What happens when you "Arrive" too soon, or when you "Arrive" too much?

- You think you have arrived, when in fact you still have more to learn.
- You rush the journey and get hurt along the way.
- You "arrive" too soon, fall asleep, and your partner gets pissed (Note: you must know your students well before you can use this one).

Now contemplate the other side of the story. A good counterpart to "Arrive" might be "Journey."

What happens when you "Journey?"

- You keep a beginner's mind and try new things.
- You embrace change.
- You look forward to a better day.

What happens when you "Journey" too much?

- You are never satisfied.
- You feel a lack of self-worth by not recognizing accomplishments.
- You might be over-efforting.

Now you have the beginnings for a *Twofold Theme*.

The best *Twofold Themes* are those where each part is a fundamental attribute that makes humans more interesting. If one side is "Good," and the other side is "Bad," you are going to have a hard time convincing your students that the "Bad" is "Good," and vice versa.

The litmus test for your word choices is that both sides of the equation could be interpreted as an *HOV*. If one side was "Arrive," and the other half was "Low Self-Esteem," or "I totally suck," you wouldn't have balance. It would still have the effect of a *One Word Theme* because only one *HOV* was relevant and able to make human beings better people.

As you contemplate the *Twofold Theme*, remember that it's not important how complicated you make it. I think the best themes are the ones that appear to be simple and true. As I like to say, what is important about a theme is not how complicated it is, or if it's an English word, or a phrase in Sanskrit. It doesn't matter if you quote Buddha or Bon Jovi or the *Bhagavad Gita*. This is the only thing that makes a theme great:

It only matters, if it matters.

Keeping in mind that it only matters if it matters, let's see what a *Twofold Theme* looks like on paper and how it will benefit your students.

Sample Theme: *Twofold Theme*

"If you lived here, you'd be home."

You: Your Yoga Branding. What is your intention in teaching?

Theme: "If you lived here, you'd be home."

HOVs: Arrive
Journey

Anecdote: On the way to work today I saw a sign that said, "If you lived here, you would be home." Instead of being on your way, you would have arrived. On the one hand, I feel I am already home in that I have accomplished many things in my life. On the other hand, I never would have seen this sign if I hadn't taken a wrong turn. Every twist and turn in our journey is there to lead us to more.

Contemplations: Arrive: Positive aspects include self-acceptance and recognition of our strengths. Being okay with getting off the bus of 'more, more, more.' The negative aspect of arriving too

soon is thinking we know all there is
to know and taking the learning
out of our journey. It closes us off
to more.
Journey: Positive aspects is it
provide continual growth and
new opportunity.
Negative: You never feel contentment
as you search for more.

Golden Nuggets:
- The journey is there to lead us to
  more.
- The journey will take us home.
  If we get lost, we might end up
  where we are supposed to be.
- One day we realize we have arrived.
- Come as you are to this party.
- You have arrived.
- Use your journey to become wiser
  along the way.
- Come inside and consider your gifts.
- Arrive at your place of contentment.
- Remember your sense of adventure
  along the way.
- Be here in the pleasure of this
  moment.

WBF:
"If we can recognize when we are
home and accomplished in our life,
but still be willing to open up to
finding more, then we will grow better
and wiser in our journey. Even getting
lost is a path to the unexpected."

| **Quotes:** | "It is better to travel well, than arrive," – Buddha "It's about the journey," some yoga teacher somewhere. |

Now your theme considers both sides of the story. If a student needs support to experiment in their practice, you can provide it. If a student needs to back off and recognize that they have achieved quite a bit, you can give them reassurance. The *Twofold Theme* is more comprehensive than a *One Word Theme*, but it did take quite a bit more work to produce.

Another benefit to the *Twofold Theme* is that if you planned a class on "Arrive," and it seemed like everyone in the room was feeling lost in their "Journey," then you could switch it up by simply changing which *Golden Nuggets* and *Quotes* you chose to emphasize. This works especially well if you planned a class on "strength," and when you showed up, it appeared that most people needed "restorative." (I have a Monday night class and it's guaranteed that whenever I plan to teach arm balances, everyone has run a marathon over the weekend!)

One word of caution: Just because you have twice as many *Golden Nuggets*, and two *HOVs* and a more involved *WBF*, it does not mean that you talk anymore in the class than you would with a *One Word Theme*.

The amount of talk never changes,
Even if you have more to say.

If you would regularly drop three to five *Golden Nuggets* in the body of your class, now you would drop half of them for "Arrive," and half for "Journey." You do not use 12 *Golden Nuggets*! You would lightly pepper your *Golden Nuggets* throughout the class just as you would in the *One Word Theme*.

At no point does our incessant talking become more important than the yoga! And this is especially true even if the theme is more complicated. A *Twofold Theme* will now be more relevant to more people, but it does not take any more time in the room away from the yoga.

Contraction and Expansion

There is one more teeny tiny little thing I would like to mention regarding the *Twofold Theme*, and I say this because it's like tip-toeing around an 800-lb gorilla.

Inside of every *Twofold Theme* lives and breathes a full-fledged, four-armed Kali-sized powerful demon capable of great destruction, or great transformation, depending on your point of view and the skill in which you can handle a theme.

If you look at your *Twofold Theme*, you will notice that one side of your new theme seems more contractive and the other feels more expansive. This is just like life, and with time we can use our themes to point out the contractive and expansive parts of our yoga. This awareness can help students deal with frustration and understand the ebb and flow of their practice, and their life off the mat.

For example, today the idea of "Arrive" feels contractive to me. If I "Arrive," I am here. I am steady. I am focused and strong. Likewise, the idea of "Journey" feels expansive to me. I am willing to try new things, expand my boundaries and go for more.

This is important: *It could be exactly the opposite depending on one's mood.* For example, the feeling of "Arrive" could be a huge expansive embrace of all that I have accomplished. And the idea of "Journey" is the work it took to get there. But for now, I'm sticking with "Arrive" being contractive, and "Journey" being expansive because I am the one writing the book.

Without getting too deep into yoga philosophy, life is made up of a contractive and expansive pulsation that is present everywhere. For example, the ocean tide goes in and out. The breath is made of an inhale and an exhale. Yoga is both strength and flexibility. Yin needs Yang. Shiva needs Shakti.

The same is true in our practice: There are contractive and expansive elements.

Examples of Pulsation in Practice:

Pose or Element

Uttanasana	Contraction: Looking inward and contracting on the exhale. Expansion: Looking outward and stretching on the inhale.
Tadasana	Contraction: Rooting to the earth, grounding down. Expansion: Lifting up and extending arms overhead.
Energy	Contraction: Muscular Energy or Inward Strength. Expansion: Organic Energy or stretching out.

As I said earlier, either "Arrive" or "Journey" could be considered the contractive or expansive part of your theme depending on your mood. For our purposes today, we will consider "Arrive" the contractive half and build a *Twofold Theme* that pulsates accordingly.

Is this necessary?

I know this sounds complicated and that some of you just jumped out the window. Honestly, you do not have to add in pulsation meaning the expansive and contractive elements to a theme. It's not necessary. Let's put this in perspective: Do you really think that by pulsating your theme you will help anyone in Headstand? I think not. Furthermore, I never, not once, ever achieved my peak pose by expanding and contracting with the theme. It was usually from practice.

However, in the right hands this is a powerful technique that can place a theme right into your students' bodies. By helping them to understand the places they need to expand, and contract, they will get a deeper awareness from yoga. Or, if you keep yammering away at them, they might leave and never come back. Pulsation is either going to be a very powerful tool for transformation, or you will destroy the students in your room by talking them to death. Who knows?

Let's see how it would look to add pulsation to our theme of "Arrive and Journey." We will link the contractive *Golden Nuggets* to "Arrive." And we will link the expansive *Golden Nuggets* to "Journey."

Here is how it might look:

Contractive Nuggets For Arrive:

- "Hug your muscles to affirm you have arrived."
- "Exhale and feel your strength inside."
- "Rooting down is a way to stand tall."
- "Steady yourself here."

Expansive Nuggets for Journey:

- "Extend outward knowing life is an adventure."
- "Inhale and expand, trusting that the journey takes you to more."
- "Rise in your Warrior and feel more opportunity in the stretch."
- "Look forward, journey to the top of your mat."

In the right hands, this could be powerful stuff. However, the yoga poses are still more important for your students. So if you are still learning your sequence and alignment cues, focusing on the pacing and managing the students, then you should probably skip this for now.

Pulsating the theme is not necessary to providing a solid class experience. It's probably good enough that you see both sides of your theme, and provide a rich verbal experience for your students. It's also great if you can see in your students where they need more emphasis in their practice so you can guide them there. Therefore, cueing this in a 90-minute class seems like a whole lot of squeeze for very little juice. That's just my opinion.

What's more, all the rules about talking too much still apply. Now that you have twice as many *Golden Nuggets*, divided among contractive and expansive moments, it still does not mean that you talk anymore in the class than you would with a *One Word Theme*! The theme, pulsated or not, is only meant to enhance a student's experience. In no way is the theme the focus of a yoga class.

The purpose of yoga is always yoga.
The inspiration is just seasoning.

So if a *Twofold Theme* with pulsation is too much seasoning, especially when you are learning to teach, do not make the stew a mess. Nothing is worse than a teacher who does not shut up. Leave all the rest of your talk to guiding students safely in and out of the poses, which is our primary responsibility as teachers.

The *Twofold Theme* Pros and Cons

Pros and Cons

Pros of using a *Twofold Theme*:
Once you are familiar with contemplating both sides of a theme, it is a more comprehensive approach. You will cast a wider net to inspire students. You will be prepared if your class turns out to be something you didn't expect. If you add in pulsation, you can connect yoga to life and to the student's body in a deep and meaningful way.

Cons of using a *Twofold Theme*:
Freaking hard. It is especially hard to pulsate the theme and not worth it except for serious "Theme Weavers." You must be able to talk without detracting from the yoga. And it's easy to switch your contractive/expansive parts and get confused. Lastly, doing this doesn't necessarily help anyone find their pose. It's a lot of squeeze for very little juice.

The *Threefold Theme*

The *Threefold Theme* is almost exactly the same as the *Twofold Theme* except that it tries to explain the place in the middle (so yogic). However, there are also *Threefold Themes* I call *Trilogy Themes* that do not explain the place in the middle (also so yogic).

The *Threefold Theme* is actually; wait for it…, easier than the *Twofold Theme*! OMG! I am not kidding. That is because of one very important dynamic: The place in the middle is going to be your *Why Bother Factor*! Hallelujah!

If the *WBF* is the hardest part of our theme to state clearly and authentically, then the *Threefold Theme* has one very distinct advantage:

The *Threefold Theme* defines the place in the middle,
Which should be the exact same reason
as why you practice yoga!

Sample Theme: The *Threefold Theme*

Let's diagram a *Threefold Theme* with "Journey" and "Arrive." If you think about it, the place in the middle of "Journey" and "Arrive," might just be "Home."

"If you lived here, you'd be home."

You: Your Yoga Branding. What is your intention in teaching?

HOV: Contractive: Arrive – Past, Accomplishments, Skills, Experience

HOV: Middle: Home – Present Moment, Knowledge, Expertise

HOV: Expansive: Journey – Future Growth, Expansion

Anecdote: "On the way to work I saw a sign that said, 'If you lived here, you would be home.' On the one hand, I feel I am already home on my mat. Yet I know I have more to learn. Every twist and turn in the road is there to teach us the path. And when we pause, we realize home is the present moment."

Contemplations: Arrive: Self-acceptance and experience. Able to recognize our strengths.
Home: The safety of home, our refuge, present moment, knowledge.

Journey: Seeing our dreams and goals and new opportunity for growth.

Golden Nuggets:
- The journey is there to show us the way.
- One day we realize we have arrived.
- We are home.
- Use your journey to become wiser along the way.
- Use your mat as home base.
- A place of acceptance.
- Look to the top of your mat.
- Jump and arrive.
- Come inside and consider your strengths.
- Arrive at contentment.
- Remember your courage along the way.
- Be here in the pleasure of this moment.
- Take a rest from your journey.
- Enjoy the present.
- You will soon journey again.
- Be here now.
- Home is this moment.

WBF: "While we spend our life journeying to new frontiers, and arriving at new skills, spend a moment recognizing that where we are now, is home. Home is where we are loved the best, and where we build our dreams for more in our lives."

Quotes:	"We shall not cease from exploration, and the end of all our exploring will be to arrive where we started and know the place for the first time." – T.S. Eliot "It is better to travel well, than arrive," – Buddha "It's about the journey," some yoga teacher somewhere. "Home is wherever we hang our hat, or roll out our mat."

A *Threefold Theme* is similar to a *Twofold Theme* except you define the place in the middle. This place is quite often where we are, or where we want to be. Or, it's like a Ping-Pong game and the middle place is where we pass through as we go back and forth in life. Either way, defining it in your *Contemplations* helps to clarify your theme, and it usually has something to do with balance, or the middle place, which are both very good things from a yoga perspective.

Lastly, if you connect this "middle place" to your Yoga Branding, you have your unique *Why Bother Factor*.

For both of these reasons, the *Threefold Theme* is actually easier to teach than the *Twofold Theme*.

The *Trilogy Theme*

The *Trilogy Theme* is like a *Threefold Theme* except that it does not have a middle place. In a *Trilogy Theme*, the three parts equally inform the other. Personally, I love the *Trilogy Theme* as it is just plain fun to teach. For example, when I theme about the three *Doshas, Vata, Kapha* and *Pitta,* my students always say they had fun, learned something and will come back. Because there isn't a clear middle place, stating the *WBF* is harder. But on the other hand, you don't have to transform someone every single time. It might be enough just to get a person on their mat and having fun.

Examples of Trilogy Themes:

- The Three Goddesses: Saraswati, Kali and Lakshmi
- The Three Gods: Brahma, Vishnu and Shiva
- The Three Doshas: Vata, Pitta and Kapha
- Three Elements: Earth, Wind and Fire
- The Three Parts of Humans: Body, Mind and Spirit

Another technique is to teach a *Trilogy Theme* over three weeks, one part at a time. Then on the fourth week, combine the three classes into one rocking event. That makes your class an experience not to be missed because everyone wants to see how the story will end.

Sample Theme: *Trilogy Theme*

Below is a sample diagram for a *Trilogy Theme*. These themes are fun to teach, but because they do not define a place in the middle the *Why Bother Factor* is frequently elusive. You can skip it, or go to 'MSU' and make something up to tie it to your Yoga Branding.

The Three Goddesses: Saraswati, Kali and Lakshmi

You: Your Yoga Branding.
What is your intention in teaching?

Theme: "The Three Goddesses"

HOVs: Saraswati is Intelligence
Kali is Transformation
Laskshmi is Beauty and Abundance

Anecdote: Each of us has parts of the three goddesses living inside us, although we may be more one than the other at certain times. When we keep a statue, or a murti of our favorite goddess, we call to her to give us strength.

Contemplations: Saraswati, the intellectual. She is smart. Too much Saraswati is too much analysis.
Kali, is the ferocious mother.
She is fierce and protective,
but sometimes she gets a little destructive.
Lakshmi, is beauty and abundance.
But sometimes she needs to step away from the mirror.

Golden Nuggets: • Step away from the mirror, Lakshmi.
• Put down the book, Saraswati.
• Ease up, Kali.

WBF:	"When we know more about who we are, we can use our gifts to become more of who we want to be."
Quotes:	"There are two types of women: Goddesses and Doormats." – Pablo Picasso "There are three types of people: the person I think I am, the people who irritate me, and the people I'd like to be." – E.M.Forster "It's never too late to be what you might have been." – George Elliot

Warning: A Cup of Shut Up

The *Trilogy* and *Threefold Themes* are among my favorite. They are intellectually provocative and keep students inspired as they sweat their way to health on the mat. But I have to be careful to keep the yoga front and center, and the theme in the background when I'm this amused or else I could just chatter on forever.

Just as when you use a *One Word Theme,* you do not talk any more when using a *Threefold Theme.* You do not take more time in the beginning or the centering. You do not stop the class to explain this very important concept of the middle place or how there isn't a middle place. Just drop a *Golden Nugget* when the time seems right to highlight a perfect moment.

If yoga is an ice cream sundae, then the theme is sprinkled on top to add sparkle, beauty, and a hint of extra sweetness to the experience.

Pros and Cons of a *Threefold Theme*

Pros and Cons

Pros of using a *Threefold Theme*:
It is easier than a *Twofold Theme* because the place in the middle is defined, and that is usually the *WBF*, which you can tie to your Yoga Brand.

Cons of using a *Threefold Theme*:
Hard to explain without talking too much.

Pros and Cons of a *Trilogy Theme*

Pros and Cons

Pros of using a *Trilogy Theme*:
Many things in life come in threes so it's a nice way to make sense of the world off our mat.

Cons of using a *Trilogy Theme*:
In some cases, harder to find the underlying *WBF* and tie it to your Yoga Brand.

The Big *Theme*

I am only going to say only a brief word about big themes, those I call the *Multi-Part Theme* with five or more components. And that's because I am generally not a fan of weekly classes with these kinds of themes because the teacher never shuts up. It becomes a lecture, not yoga. There are some teachers who can weave a big *Multi-Part Theme* beautifully. But many, sadly, do not. And not once did it actually change my practice or my life off the mat.

The big *Multi-Part Theme* could be about anything but is often based on the *bandhas*, the *tattvas*, the *chakras* or the *Yoga Sutras*. And this is how it sounds to your students:

"Waa, Waaaaaa, Waa, Waaaaaa Waa Waaaaaa."

If you don't believe me, ask your students after class which of the *tattvas* they most related to, and they will look at you with a blank stare.

I recommend teaching these large, *Multi-Part Themes* in a three-hour or weekend workshop. However, although difficult, it's not impossible to tackle a large subject in a weekly class. If you want to teach on the *Yamas* and *Niyamas,* for example, I recommend doing so one at a time and treat them like a *One Word Theme*. Or, take two of the *Sutras* and teach them as a *Twofold Theme*. For example, *Santosha*—contentment with *Tapas*—desire to improve. They balance each other nicely in a theme.

If you want to teach the *chakras*, as another example, then perhaps try to focus on one at a time. Another approach is to balance two with each other such as *Manipura*, which is near the core and is considered the center of dynamism and achievement, with *Anahata* the heart, where we try to act purely for the sake of love.

The key is to make the big *Multi-Part Theme* matter to your students, and to do so in a way that improves their practice, and motivates them to make a change in their life.

A theme only matters if it matters, and if it reflects on how we become better human beings off the mat. Keep that in mind, and you will not get lost along the way.

"You cannot plough a field by
turning it over in your mind."
Author Unknown

The Multi-Part Theme Standard Format

You: Write your Yoga Branding at the top of every Sheet.

Theme: State your phrase or concept.

HOVs: Contractive
Expansive
Middle Place

The *Human Operating Value* is the fundamental quality that makes us better, and is underlying the meaning of the class. Pulsating is optional. If you are using a *Trilogy*, or a *Multi-Part Theme*, you may not have a middle place. So be it.

Anecdote: A story or phrase or narrative that sets the tone and provides imagery for the class. It must be succinct, universalized and related to yoga and life. Even though it sets up a bigger theme, it still must be completed in time to honor the rule, "Five Minutes to the Move."

Contemplate: Journal to understand what the theme means to you. Consider what happens with too much, and too little of each *HOV*. This should reveal the "middle place" and some excellent *Golden Nuggets*.

Golden Nuggets: Tidbits and phrases you create from your *Contemplations* which you drop throughout the class. These lend inspiration and motivation to the theme. Even though you may have three, or a big *Multi-Part Theme,* you do not talk more than in using a *One Word Theme.* You just divide the *Golden Nuggets* between the concepts.

WBF: The *Why Bother Factor* tells students why they should care and practice yoga. It connects the *Theme* to your Yoga Branding, and makes it a unique experience from every other teacher's offering.

In the *Multi-Part Theme* the middle place may not be defined, so you might want to make up a *WBF* that ties to your Yoga Brand.

Quote: The *Quote* is the cherry on top. Use it at the beginning, or the end, but be sure to pause after saying it so the students can take it in. Either find a *Quote,* or use a strong mnemonic phrase they can remember and take with them off the mat.

Chapter Six

Tie It Together

"Oh what a tangled web we weave,
When first we practice to deceive."
~ Shakespeare

When I first began teaching, I made the mistake many new teachers make: I was way too ambitious. Peers reviewed me and every single one said the same thing: Holy Cow! (Some were not that nice.)

From my first days in the room I had a *Threefold Theme*, pulsated, and connected to a peak pose. I built the pose sequentially using a specific physical action. I used props and partnering exercises. And I would never, ever shut up. My students panted like rabbits trying to keep up.

And the end result was not a great yoga class, but a hot mess. Without organization and focus, my students suffered and I didn't grow as a teacher either.

The last step to becoming a "Theme Weaver," where we connect the power of inspiration to perspiration, is to construct our class so that all the parts work together: The theme, the sequence, the physical actions, the adjustments, and the props. Remember, you are creating not just a class, but a total experience for your students that they will not want to miss.

The Sequence

In the challenge of becoming a new teacher, I was told to guide the same exact, same physical sequence for 25 classes while working on my themes and everything else. This advice saved me.

Those of us who teach any kind of a set sequence such as Bikram's Hot Yoga sequence, or a beginner's sequence have a huge advantage. It's one less thing to worry about in the room. You can be more skillful with your theme because your brain is not (excessively) occupied with where to go next.

If you do not have the security of teaching a set sequence, then you have the luxury of choosing your own. I would still recommend creating a structure and staying with it until you feel comfortable with all the other moving parts of a class. This may take a week, or a few months. Only you will know when you are ready to move on. Remember, the Ashtanga yogis have stayed with the same set sequences for about 2,000 years, and they seem to be doing just fine.

When you put together a class, it does not matter if you start by choosing the poses you want to teach, or the theme you want to express. But once you have chosen, you will want to match your sequence and theme so they both work toward the same experience.

For example, you would not want to choose a posture sequence that calls for intense focus and clarity when you theme about "surrender." It's really not a good time to just let everything go when you are in one-armed Handstand! Likewise, nothing drives me more bat-shit crazy than a class on building strength, and the poses are restorative.

For our class on "Arrive and Journey," we focused on self-acceptance and being open to learning more. You would want to pick a pose that is accessible to most students with modifications if necessary. It's a pretty crummy feeling to be listening to a theme on how you are good enough, and then be the only one in the room who can't do the pose.

Know Your Audience

When you go about creating your class, it is also critically important to know your audience. Christina Sell, founder of the San Marcos School of Yoga and the author of two books on yoga, says that every class has three types of students:

- The Engineer. The Engineer is a student who wants to know exactly where to put his left elbow or his right knee. They love the technical guidance. They are yoga-nerds and want all the alignment details. Cue them precisely and they are happy.

- The Mystic. The Mystic is a student who loves the spiritual part of yoga, the themes, the stories and the part of the practice that connects to our spirit. They could lie on their back in *Savasana* the whole time if you just tell them a story about Ganesha. These students are attracted to Theme Weavers.

- The Athlete: The Athlete wants to move. This student decides how good the class is by the size of the puddle of sweat left on the mat. They do not want to hear about any spiritual crap. They want you to shut up, so they can push up.

Because aspects of each of these types of students exist in each of us, a skillful teacher will balance the class sequence and the theme for all three. So if you notice that you are talking a lot about your theme, add in some sit-ups for your athletes. If you have been doing a lot of *Chaturangas*, or push-ups, add in a break and a *Golden Nugget* for your mystics. If you've been calling the name of the poses and the breath, pause and add in some specific alignment cues for your engineers. That way you keep everyone engaged and motivated.

In addition, be conscious of who is in your room. If you have lots of young dudes, do not theme constantly about the challenge of aging. Find different *Golden Nuggets* to keep everyone interested and engaged in your class.

Teaching the Physical Cues

In addition to selecting a *Theme*, *HOV* and sequence of poses, the next thing to figure out is what you want to teach about your class physically or energetically. Yoga is an endless vortex with a million things to learn about each pose. Yet a typical mistake is to unload on our students all the things we know at once. And this is how it sounds to our students:

"Waa, Waaaaaa, Waa, Waaaaaa Waa Waaaaaa."

I know you are brilliant. You know you are brilliant. But it is best to put aside everything you have learned and just teach your students one or two things in a class. That is all a human being will remember anyway.

The choices are infinite on what physical or energetic aspect of yoga you may want to teach on a particular day. You might choose to teach about core support. Or you might have been working on the placement of the hands and feet over a span of a few weeks. However, another way to decide is to pick an element that supports your *Theme.*

For example, if I am using the theme "Arrive" as an example of confidence and with a contractive flavor, I might choose to teach physical concepts that help students to feel grounded. Therefore, I might instruct rooting down to the earth, engaging muscular strength or using the core to create stability. It would seem confusing to teach about lifting or extending if everything I'm saying is to create steadiness and a feeling of having 'arrived.'

On the other hand, if I am teaching a theme about "Journey" as an example of growing and extending ourselves with an expansive flavor, I might teach physical cues which create extension. I might suggest organically stretching in each pose, filling the back of the body to create a feeling of lift, or an energetic concept of feeling supported by a greater power.

The list is endless of physical or energetic ways to teach yoga. But try to match the intention of your theme to the intention in your body. This places the theme right inside your students where they can feel it the most. What isn't necessary is to teach like a yoga-robot and continually cue the same old things about the hands and feet, or about reaching for the sky or whatever you say unless it illuminates your current class.

If the cues don't light up the theme,
Or the meaning of your class,
Then don't use them.

How do you find out if you are using too many cues? Ask your students after class what feels different in their body or in their practice. If they can't tell you, it's because they may have tuned you out. Try to stick to poses that support the theme, and an alignment concept that builds to a single-pointed focus for the class. Then students will probably 'get it.' If not, there's always next time!

Adjusting for the Theme

Plenty of great teachers have been burned by adjustments. It is the number one way to change a student's practice and help them change something in their body. And it is the number one way to hurt someone. The balance of risk and reward in giving adjustments is high stakes, and it may not always be worth it.

Although some yoga schools preach that every student should be touched in every class, I am not a believer in that philosophy. Students may have come to class just to practice and not be harped on. You might learn this lesson by entering a student's space to offer some very helpful guidance, and instead they burst into tears or yell at you. Um, maybe it wasn't a good day?

There are also days when you shouldn't be offering adjustments because you are not in a great place. I have been adjusted by an angry teacher, and I've also been adjusted by a teacher who started crying on top of me! Not my mess, but now the teacher has made it mine to clean up. And don't even get me started about being touched by the teacher who is sneezing and wiping her runny nose. *Om Namah Shivaya!*

However, if you are in a good place, and you've sensitively assessed that your students are in a good place, then here are my two cents on adjusting.

Know what you want to do
Before you do it.

I believe that many teachers struggle with adjustments because they've been taught how to do it before they've been taught how to see the student. For example, yoga teacher training traditionally focuses on how many adjustments we can memorize for a pose. So for Warrior Two, you can kneel and adjust the hips, or you can extend the arms, or you gently move the front knee outward, or you can fix the feet, or you can encourage the shoulder blades down the back, blah, blah, blah.

Wrong.

What if you had a purpose before you moved into a student's space and began changing them? What if your purpose was your theme? *OMG!*

If you are teaching "Arrive" as a grounding experience expressing confidence and self-acceptance, then you would want to choose the adjustments that enhance that feeling. You want students to feel grounded, complete and secure. In Warrior Two, choose the adjustments that would help them feel rooted. For example, you might gently press down on the hips. Or you might call attention to the feet and make their foundation more stable. In *Tadasana*, you might adjust in a similar way by again holding a student's hips and gently pushing down. This reinforces the message that we are strong and good enough just as we are.

When you are reinforcing steadiness, it is not a good time to lift them up by the arms to reach further. Right? Because if you are teaching that they are good enough as they are, why would you lift them out of their space?

On the other hand, if you are teaching a theme based on "Journey" as an expanding feeling of reaching beyond boundaries, this is an excellent time to extend a student in a pose. You might adjust Warrior Two by gently holding the wrists and encouraging the arms outward. Or, you might extend a student by gently lifting up her ribcage. In *Tadasana*, if you hold a student's hips, I would verbalize that she should stretch up. Or, I might gently extend her arms upward.

By matching the adjustment to your theme, you have another opportunity to create a meaningful experience for your students. You don't have to remember what kind of adjustment goes with a certain pose, just remember what you are trying to create for your students and the idea for an adjustment will come naturally.

By knowing what you want to do,
You will figure out what you should do.

Don't Forget Your Props

The props you choose to use in your class are just like every other part of the experience: they must work with the theme! Props are not there for our amusement. They shouldn't be used just to take up some time or to try something new (unless your theme is to try something new!). They should be introduced just like everything else: to build to a single point of focus for the class.

Nothing drives me crazier when I am on my mat and a teacher pulls out a prop and asks us to use it in a way that does not support the intention of the class. For example, the class is on surrendering and softening, and the teacher asks us to use a strap in *Chaturanga. OMG*, that is hard! There is no surrender there at all. Or, we are asked to balance on a block, but the *Theme* is, "Find sweetness in life." Right? Using the block to find sweetness, is like looking for gold in an oil well: Wrong time, wrong place.

When you introduce a prop, be aware that you are interrupting the students' practice. You are stopping the *asana, pranayama*, and the focus on intention. So it better be good. Please don't pull something out that you just saw on YouTube because it looked cool. No, it is not cool. It is distracting.

If your use of a prop does not further the students' understanding of the physical actions you are teaching, or of the theme, or to answer a question they had, or because they need help, then it was a waste of their time. If you consistently waste students' time, they will not come back to yoga. They will go outside and enjoy the day instead.

To use props mindfully, you might try using a block between the shins to encourage muscular engagement and steadiness in a grounding theme. If you are teaching expansion, then have them face a wall and press into it for Warrior Three. The possibilities are endless, but be mindful in choosing.

Everything you do, everything you teach should be aligned with your intention for the class to create a cohesive experience for the students.

A Word on Organization

Finally, the effort you put into creating your classes will provide the big payoff: less work in the future to teach a consistently amazing class.

So far, becoming a "Theme Weaver" has been a lot of work. You've had to decide who you are, and why you teach. You've created a Yoga Bio, Mission Statement and Yoga Branding. As if one "Eight Limbed Path" wasn't enough, you became acquainted with the "Other Eight Limbed Path" to create themes. Finally, you are matching your sequence, physical actions, energetic cues, adjustments and props all to create a single point of focus for your students.

Now you get to enjoy the rewards of all that work.

No More Getting Lost in the Woods

There is a long-running joke in my family. Whenever we are lost in the car or hiking in the woods and become totally turned around, I would say to the kids, "Don't worry. We are on an adventure now."

It wasn't long before the word "adventure" became synonymous with "Uh oh."

It is the same in our classes. Who hasn't been there when the class took a wrong turn and became a big adventure? Or when you are ready to teach 'Drop Backs' and the students who showed up cannot do a Cobra pose?

There are always times when good classes go bad. Those are the days I say, okay today we're going to go upside down. Because who wants to listen to a theme balancing on their heads?

However, there is a better way and it's called organization.

By knowing what you want to do,
You will figure out what you should do.

Build Your Theme Library

Organization is your way to protect against an adventure going bad.

How you choose to store your themes is personal. One of my teachers creates his classes in notebooks which he stores on a bookshelf. Although they all look black and white to me, he is able to pull one out of the bunch and instantly find what he is looking for. That works for him.

I use a computer to store my themes. I have more than 300 classes created based on *Themes*, and posture sequences. Personally, I store my posture sequences separately. Then, when it is time to teach, I print a separate page for my *Theme* and one for my *asana* sequence to mix and match them.

One week I might teach a *One Word Theme* of "Surrender" with *Urdhva Dhanurasana*, wheel pose. Then the next time, I might teach "Surrender" with a hip-opening sequence. They would be two very different classes. If you are eco-conscious, you could download the theme sheets to your tablet or computer and bring that into the room instead of a paper copy. The question is, what will work for you?

Organization is the Key to Success

Storing your work is as important as creating it, and being able to find a *Theme* quickly saves you time and effort in planning classes.

For example, you see a sign on the road that says, "If you lived here, you'd be home." You know you are feeling less than grounded these days and that is what you want to teach. All you have to do is pull out the last time you taught a grounding concept, or a *Theme* based on "stability" as your *HOV*, update it with the new *Anecdote*, and you are good to go. You already have *Golden Nuggets* on the topic, and a *Quote* and *WBF*. The new theme should take less than three minutes to complete.

There are many ways you might organize your *Themes*. In my case, I store them based on *HOVs* such as:

- Surrender
- Hope
- Desire
- Strength

When I settle on a mood for the class, I only need to look up a *Theme* I used in a similar situation. I change a few words, make it fresh and relevant, and I'm ready to go. So the week my son and I both had very unexpected surgery, I chose a *Theme* from the 'Hope' category called, "When Things Fall Apart."

If I choose to plan a class around the concept of surrendering, I go to my 'Surrender' file, and look at the individual *Themes*. I pick the nearest one to my present mood, and then modify and update it. That "Theme Sheet" will already have my past *Contemplations*, *HOV* and synonyms, *Anecdotes*, *Golden Nuggets*, a *WBF* and *Quotes*. I can use the existing material, or update it. Now it's ready to go for a new class.

It Gets Easier

In the beginning, it will probably take some time and effort to create your classes. But it pays off handsomely in the end with consistently prepared teaching no matter what life throws at you and believe me, life will throw some crazy stuff at you!

The Time It Takes to Create a Theme and its Components:
- The first time: Approximately one hour.
- The second time you revise it to make it fresh: Approximately 15 minutes.
- The "emergency" class: 15 seconds to print and/or remember.

Pros and Cons of Being an Ultimate Theme Weaver

Pros of being a "Theme Weaver:"
It connects the power of inspiration to teaching yoga, and transforms the students in your class. The class is now a cohesive experience. If students don't understand why they should do something physically, they might comprehend it if you tie it to their desire to live a more full and satisfying life. It distinguishes you as an outstanding teacher and keeps your classes full with eager students. It gives you many ways to motivate someone on the mat.

Cons of being a "Theme Weaver:"
Ridiculously hard. Makes good yoga teachers doubt themselves. Requires lots of preparation and mental stamina. Often results in constant chatter.
Remember, yoga is all our students need. But yoga with a helping of inspiration is even better.

Summary

Once upon a time, I was an excellent yoga teacher.

Then I began to doubt myself. Several advanced teacher trainings later led me to believe that I was, in fact, a terrible teacher. Some days I questioned whether or not I even wanted to go into the room anymore.

But little by little, the clouds began to part and I saw the benefit of connecting the power of inspiration to teaching yoga. I created the concept of "Theme Weaver" and I became steadier on my feet and in my seat as the teacher. I saw my students grow and transform before my eyes. I was hearing that the practice was changing them mind, body and soul. And I realized that I was indeed, a pretty terrific teacher.

Just like yoga, teaching is a practice too. We have good days, and some not so good days.

But I believe that if our intention is to deliver the highest quality class we can, and if we make the effort, then it has to be better than if we didn't try at all. Even the days we fall short will probably be good days for our students. No effort is ever wasted.

Mythology tells us that the Hindu God Ganesha was the first "Theme Weaver." He recorded the battle in the *Bhagavad Gita*.

He dipped his broken tusk into a river of blood to write the words that would forever inspire yogis, on and off the mat.

Like Ganesha, you will also write the most beautiful classes, even if you have to dip your pen into a pool of tears from your efforts. I wish you joy along your journey and just enough suffering so that you get better. Know that wherever you roll out your mat, or take your seat as the teacher, no effort is ever wasted. Know that you are already good enough because you showed up for your students. Doubt your doubts, because even if you don't already know it, you have arrived.

If you lived here, in the seat of the teacher, you'd be home now.

Namaste.

APPENDICES

A. To Theme Or Not To Theme – FAQs

B. What Drives Students Crazy? Survey Says

C. 10 Things You Can Do To Improve

D. Frequent Fliers: Themes At Your Fingertips

E. Common Human Operating Values

F. Where To Find Some Instant Inspiration

G. Stupid Things Smart Yoga Teachers Say

H. Recommended Resources

To Theme Or Not To Theme – FAQs

Q: **Do I have to theme my class?**

A: Absolutely not.

Q: **Are there times when it is appropriate not to theme a class?**

A: Yes! Yoga does not really need a theme. It's perfectly fine to let the *asana* do the work of transforming students. Please do not try to theme if you are upset, not in the mood, or just didn't want to teach.

For example, once I was checking in my class and my phone rang. I answered it, and received some sad news. I began to cry and then from little sniffles it went to great big sobs. The more I tried to stop, the harder I cried. Ten minutes later I walked into the room, still crying, and this is what I said: "I am all right. My family is all right. I received some bad news, but in the big scheme of things, we are going to be okay. However, we are just going to get through this class the best we can."

I led them through a sequence one step, one breath at a time. Many students came up to me afterward and said they were struck by how steady the class had been. That is much better than trying to theme. But the moral of the story is, do not answer your phone just before you teach.

Q: **Do I have to theme on two things? I can barely theme on one.**

A: A *One Word Theme* is perfectly fine. However, if you do a single *Theme*, like a phrase, I would recommend connecting it to an underlying *HOV* or else it may feel trite.

Q: **I can theme, but the *Why Bother Factor* is really hard. Do I have to do it?**

A: The *WBF* is the hardest part of "The Other Eight Limb Path." But, it is where you connect the *Theme* to your unique Yoga Brand. If you are unclear about why you teach, then the *WBF* will be impossible. That's why I call the *WBF* the "smell test." If you can't say it with conviction, go back and see if the whole theme reeks of insincerity.

Practice makes it easier. Pretend you are telling someone why yoga will change their life. If you still can't state a *WBF*, then skip it. The world is not going to end and your students will probably reach enlightenment anyway.

Q: **I can do a *Twofold Theme* with two *HOVs*, but do I have to pulsate it?**

A: No. Honey, you don't even need to theme. It took me years of practice before I felt ready to pulsate it. And even though I am a "Theme Weaver," there are many days when I don't (and my students seem abnormally happy).

Q: **I can't do many of the advanced poses. Do I have to be able to do them to teach them?**

A: Some say yes. Some say no. I am in the maybe camp. On the one hand, there are poses I cannot yet do but feel comfortable teaching because I know exactly how to cue someone into them. But if you don't know the first thing about how to get there, I might stick with what you do know for now. You'll come off as more authentic to your students and attract students who will grow with you.

Q: **What if I planned a class on "vigor" and everyone seems pooped?**

A: Great question. I might try to talk about the need for vigor. Or, I might try to switch on the fly to something restorative. If you planned your class with a dual theme, such as the benefits of both vigor and restoration, then you would be covered.

Q: **My teacher wants me to theme using historic Sanskrit texts, and I'm just not feeling it.**

A: If a theme doesn't speak to you, then by all means, don't use it. A theme is only as good as you can deliver it. Speak from the concepts in your Mission Statement and you will be fine.

Q: **Can I teach if I am injured and can't do the poses?**

A: Yes. In fact, you will probably be better at weaving the theme and watching your students. One of my favorite teachers had a broken foot and was in a cast for six weeks. Her teaching was never better than at this time. She gave us her full attention even if she couldn't walk around.

Q: **Can I theme just at the beginning and end of class?**

A: Why? So you can take up the student's time and have it have no meaning in their bodies? The purpose of the theme is to enlighten the practice and place intention in the body. So why skip the middle? No theme is better than the theme sandwich approach. Also in this category is saying a quote and not relating it to your class. Ugh. Spare us.

Q: **Is it okay to start with one *Theme*, and then switch to another if it sounds good?**

A: No. Or maybe. If you start with "Arrive," and end up with "Feel Comfortable at Home," you are still in the same ballpark. But if you start with "Arrive," and end up at "Surrender," you took a wrong turn and brought your students along for the ride. Stick to one theme per class so your students can understand it and find more in their practice. It takes five to seven mentions in an hour for them to even hear it once. You owe it to them to stay on point.

Q: **Should we theme at all? Is it right to force our agenda on a yoga student?**

A: Good question. I hope you are choosing themes that can be tied to a *Human Operating Value*, and hopefully one that will make us better, wiser and stronger. If you are choosing themes like hatred, resentment and disgust, you might need to go back to Yoga 101.

If you are choosing themes like courage, confidence and trust, you will help your students feel better. If you are choosing themes about being vegan or who to vote for in an election, it might seem like an agenda so be careful. Lastly, if you teach a pure sequence once in a while without a theme, it will provide a nice relief as well.

Q: **After class my strong students feel great, but my weaker students feel terrible. What can I do?**

A: Good for you for noticing! First of all, consider your word choices. I had a teacher who would say, "A good student will jump switch." Well, I am a good student with arthritis, so I don't often jump switch. But I can understand that after hearing this for an hour, I might feel 'less than' after class. Watch your speech and see if you can help with encouraging word choices.

What Drives Students Crazy?

Showing up late. Or unprepared, or not at all!

Too much talk. This is the most annoying thing we do after not showing up! Add depth without disruption. Let the *asana* take center stage.

Weak themes. *Themes, Quotes* and *Anecdotes* used indiscriminately throughout the class and a lack of *Contemplation* to tie it together.

No Human Operating Values. Nothing substantial or meaningful in the theme – it's just a catchphrase or yoga jargon.

Switching horses. Jumping from *Theme* to *Theme* or tossing around multiple *HOVs* is like switching horses in the middle of a race. This includes dropping any stupid thoughts that just popped into our head. Put a filter on it.

The theme sandwich. Starting and ending with a *Theme*, but using no *Golden Nuggets* in the middle. It has no meaning for the students and doesn't transform their practice. Skip the *Theme* completely instead.

Yoga gobbledygook. This includes clichés, overused quotes, and anything about letting go.

Unsafe *asana* sequencing. For example, being asked to do a backbend without having opened the quads. Or using a difficult posture in a flow sequence. It's time to take care of our students, people, so other people can stop saying that yoga is unsafe.

What Does Not Drive Students Crazy?

Not having a theme! Never have I heard a student complain that the teacher didn't have a theme. Not once. If you don't feel like theming, then skip it and teach *asana* instead.

10 Things You Can Do To Improve

1. **Get on your mat.**

   Nothing improves your teaching like practice. Nothing. But we become a teacher, and suddenly we are racing from class to class never finding time to get on our mat. Make time for yourself. Take care of yourself.

2. **Get a journal.**

   Contemplation is the single most important thing you can do in preparing classes.

3. **Get an attitude.**

   Nothing will give your students more confidence than if you have confidence in yourself. It is delightfully infectious. If you cue with authority, theme with integrity and take your seat as the teacher, your students will give you their trust.

4. **Get rid of the attitude.**

   On the other hand, nothing will empty your yoga room faster than having too much of an attitude. It's never a good idea to believe your own P.R. The only reason we are in the room is to serve our students.

5. **Teach to your students.**

   Be aware of your audience. Speak to everyone and prepare a sequence that will appeal to everyone at some point.

6. **Keep "you" in balance.**

   We all have issues, but when we teach, it is not the time to work them out. You are here to serve. You are not here to practice, or to air your problems, or to show everyone how amazing you are. Keep the talk and demos to a minimum. Keep *Anecdotes* about the students by saying, "Has this ever happened to you?" Remember, you are not the "doer." You are a revealer or a guide.

7. **Go back to school.**

   The more we teach, the more we learn. The more we learn, the better we teach. Continue your education. The teacher who is a student first, is always a better teacher.

8. **Read.**

   You are not Shiva in a mountain cave. I once attended a yoga class the day the Denver Nuggets basketball team made the playoffs, and we were all excited. The teacher said, "What's a Nugget?" Come on, really? Join us in the present world, please.

9. **Write your Mission Statement.**

   If you don't know why you are teaching, nobody else will either. Be clear about your purpose and you will be clear in your message.

10. **Have fun and be yourself.**

    If you are not having any fun, ain't nobody gonna have any fun. Be yourself, share from the heart and your students will have permission to do the same.

Frequent Flyers: Themes At Your Fingertips

While no one *Theme* is right for everyone, these concepts form the basis for a comprehensive library. They are versatile and speak to many students on some level. Prepare a theme sheet on each of these subjects in a way that speaks to you. If you prefer a *One Word Theme*, then create classes on each of these words. Over time see if you can put two classes together and move toward a *Twofold Theme*.

Arrive and Journey

Effort and Surrender

Stability and Freedom

Desire and Manifestation

Planning and Spontaneity

Individual and Universal

Finding the Light and Appreciating the Dark

The *Yamas* and *Niyamas*

The Yoga Sutras by Patanjali

Appendix E

Common Human Operating Values

Human Operating Values, or the emotions, feelings and sentiments that make us human, are the foundation of any great yoga class. These intentions would serve as the basis for a *One Word Theme,* or you could compare two for a *Twofold Theme.*

This is by no means a complete list.

HOVs that might be considered with a contractive implication

Recognition	Wisdom	Mindfulness	Discernment
Steadfastness	Stability	Resolution	Remembrance
Effort	Faith	Trust	Believe
Courage	Fearlessness	Confidence	Resilience
Vigor	Desire	Practice	Devotion
Individual	Self-Love	Self-Respect	Integrity

HOVs that might be considered with an expansive implication

Surrender	Yielding	Generosity	Offering
Non-Harming	Non-Judging	Non-Clinging	Happiness
Compassion	Kindness	Love	Joy
Acceptance	Freedom	Spontaneity	Playfulness
Silence	Harmony	Humility	Gratitude

Appendix F

Where To Find Some Instant Inspiration

Social Media

Social Media is an unlimited source for inspiration. There are a number of people who tweet and post inspiration all day long. I have been inspired by Cora Wen, Amy Ippoliti, Christina Sell and even Oprah on Twitter. Other good bets are Rumi (apparently he has a Twitter account), Darren Rhodes, Bernadette Birney and YogaGlo. Twitter feeds are restricted to 160 characters, so that will help keep you brief and succinct as well.

Internet Media

There are multiple news outlets on the Internet which focus on yoga. Try *The Daily Om, Yoga Journal, Yogadork, The Yoga Blog, Teachasana, My Yoga Online, Elephant Journal* and countless more. The blogs are sure to spark a fire in you.

Books

There are a number of writers who focus on yoga or Eastern Religion. Try Judith Lasater, Eckhart Tolle, Pema Chodron, B.K.S. Iyengar, Baron Baptiste, Georg Feuerstein, Deepak Chopra and Christina Sell. My book, *Finding More on the Mat: How I Grew Better, Wiser and Stronger through Yoga,* is actually 18 chapters, each focused on a yoga theme.

Yoga Texts

Your library should include: *The Bhagavad Gita, Ramayana, Mahabharata, The Yoga Sutras* by Patanjali and *Light on Yoga and Light on Life* by B.K.S. Iyengar.

Hindu Mythology

The Hindu stories and myths of the Gods are rich in metaphor and theme ideas. Two good resources are *Myths of the Asanas* by Alanna Kaivalya and *Indian Mythology* by Paul Hamlyn. Another is the Internet. One caveat: there is usually more than one interpretation of a myth, so choose the version that speaks to you, and then cite your source to CYA: *Cover-your-asana.*

Television, Movies, Etc.

You can find nuggets of inspiration in your daily life. *Good Morning America* did a segment on transforming an everyday person into a supermodel. That was the basis for my *Theme*: "Your Inner Supermodel." The movie, *The Legend of Bagger Vance*, is a retelling of the *Bhagavad Gita.* Anything can be inspirational, if you feel inspired by it.

Holidays, Seasons and Nature

Holidays, anniversaries, the changing of seasons, solstice days and weather are all opportunities for themes. One forewarning: if you are going to theme about love on Valentine's Day, be aware that just about every other yoga teacher is doing the same thing.

Your Mat

Your yoga practice will tell you just about anything you need to know about life. Get on your mat, and then speak to your experience. Your students will love it.

Appendix G

Stupid Things Smart Yoga Teachers Say

The anal-obsessed comments. I'm thinking we should let this stuff go.

- "Pretend there is a flashlight in your butt and shine it to the stars." Really?
- "Relax your anal mouth." Ewwwww, just plain gross.
- "Relax your anus." Do not!
- "Every breath starts in the pelvic floor, that's why tight ass people don't know how to breathe."
- "Engage your perineum." I'm not sure it can be engaged.
- "When in doubt, stick it out." Guilty!

When not in your own body, or your right mind.

- 'Yoga Voice.' It is distracting. Yoga voice is a sing-song, la-di-da kind of voice which undermines the theme and everything you have to say. Please speak normally.
- Jargon that is not yours. Everyone will know, but most of all, you will feel like a phony.

Jargon and clichés. Really, nobody knows what Earth you are talking about.

- "Lift from your Gracillis, or Semimembranosus." Any location on the body needs to be pointed out and explained for a directional cue to have meaning. You can't assume your class took anatomy. I sometimes say, "Leg butt." But who knows what that is either? Point to it!

- "Inner Body Bright," "Spiral" anything, anywhere and "Side-bodies." Jargon sounds like nonsense. Please say, "The side of your body," at least once and point to what you mean.

- "Find your way to the front of the mat." What? Am I lost?

- "High to the sky." Beware of overdoing rhymes. If the rhyme don't fit, you may need to acquit.

- "Just Breathe." This also includes: "Big breath in." When you have something real to say, you will find less of a need to depend on clichés.

- "Just let go." Of what? Honestly, I want to scream when I hear it.

And just plain stupid.

- "Close your eyes from top to bottom."

- "Lift your chins."

- "Picture a bright light flowing through your nostrils; let your eyes rest in your sockets like bobbers; let your butt blossom towards the back of the room, firm but flexible; just breathe."

- "Engage and soften." At the same time?

- "Drink from the blessed water." We're in the Vatican now?

- "Rock it like Ganesha." He rocks? I think he rolls.

- "Let go of your orgasm toes." Probably a good idea to let go of the orgasm talk in class.

- "Here's a quote from Rumi." (Insert irrelevant, un-contemplated and esoteric Rumi quote here, and then don't mention it again in class.)

- "One time at yoga camp." There's a yoga camp? Can I sign up?

- "Mr. Iyengar told me that....." Yeah, right.

Recommended Resources

Brand Thyself with Jess, by Jessica Boylston-Fagonde
(*www.BrandThyself.com*) A yoga professional with marketing
skills and a therapeutic approach for discovering your unique
yoga brand.

90 Monkeys, by Amy Ippoliti (*www.AmyIppoliti.com* or
www.90monkeys.com) Workshops, webinars and social media
support designed to improve yoga instructors who take their
profession seriously.

Light on Yoga, and Light on Life, by B.K.S. Iyenger (Schocken
Books) and *Light on the Yoga Sutras of Patanjali,* by B.K.S.
Iyengar (Thorsons Publishers). Mr. Iyengar is the premier
resource for all things yoga, and every teacher should have
these books in their library.

Yoga from the Inside Out, and *My Body is a Temple,* by
Christina Sell (Hohm Press). My inspiration and literary
mentor, Christina Sell, blends virtue with *asana.*

Living Your Yoga, by Judith Lasater (Rodmell Press). What yoga
looks like off the mat.

Meditations from the Mat, by Rolf Gates and Katrina Kenison,
(Anchor Books). Inspiration for yoga.

Journey into Power, by Baron Baptiste, (Fireside).
An introduction to the power of yoga, and Power Yoga.

The Bhagavad Gita, any translation. How to live with *dharma,* integrity and divine inspiration.

The Mahabharata and *Ramayana,* any translation.
Historic texts filled with metaphor and mythology.

The Yoga Tradition, by Georg Feuerstein (Hohm Press).
The ultimate, comprehensive book on yoga.

Yoga Gems, by Georg Feuerstein (Bantam Press).
Filled with yoga wisdom.

When Things Fall Apart and other books by Pema Chodrin, (Shambahala Library). My go-to resource for spiritual guidance.

Nourishing the Teacher, by Danny Arguetty (Arguetty).
Advice for keeping yoga teachers fed spiritually.

Finding More on the Mat: How I Grew Better, Wiser and Stronger through Yoga, by Michelle Berman Marchildon (Wildhorse Ventures). Every chapter is a theme revealing how it relates to life and yoga.

Previous Books by the Author

Finding More on the Mat: How I Grew Better, Wiser and Stronger through Yoga (2012, Wildhorse Ventures) is a modern-day yoga fairy tale about a woman who stumbled into her first yoga class by accident, and discovered a path to have a great second half of her life. Laced with humor and honest transparency that is inspiring to people both on and off the mat, Michelle shows how yoga is more than the funny postures you see; it's a chance to hold ourselves in the belief that we can be more, not less, at any age, with any circumstance in our lives.

What People are Saying

"Michelle's honest, warm and inviting story is a must-read for anyone seeking to find their truth through the practice of yoga. Growing older gracefully is no easy task, and *Finding More on the Mat* reminds us that we are not walking the path alone and that true wisdom and strength can only be found through dedicated efforts over the course of our lives. May this story inspire and bless your efforts."

> – Christina Sell, bestselling author of *Yoga from the Inside Out: Making Peace with your Body through Yoga* and *My Body is a Temple: Yoga as a Path to Wholeness.*

"In a style similar to Elizabeth Gilbert's "Eat, Pray, Love," Michelle reveals her own version of the life story that many of us have experienced on our way to discovering inner peace and inner strength. I laughed out loud while reading this book and at the same time, the words touched my soul because I saw myself as she shared her personal experience. Whether you practice yoga or not, reading this book will help you understand why it is being practiced by millions of people in the world. This is one of the most inspirational and timely books on yoga in the world today. We need this book!"

– Desiree Rumbaugh, Certified Yoga Teacher and creator of the *Yoga to the Rescue* DVD series.

About the Author

Michelle Berman Marchildon is the Yogi Muse. She is an award-winning journalist and an E-RYT 500 Hatha Yoga Teacher with Yoga Alliance. She is the author of the best-selling memoir, *Finding More on the Mat: How I Grew Better, Wiser and Stronger through Yoga*. Her work has been featured in *Elephant Journal, Origin Magazine, Yoga Journal, My*  *Yoga Online* and *Teachasana*. She lives in Denver, Colorado, where she is raising two boys, two dogs and one husband.

Michelle's mission is to help everyone find more out of life, starting on the mat. Through a balance of alignment and flow, Michelle's classes take you deeper in your practice to rediscover your potential. Known as the "Theme Weaver," Michelle puts intention into action to give you a path to find your dreams. She believes that through the steady practice of yoga, everyone can find more in their lives.

You can download her classes from *www.YogaDownload.com*.
For more information and her schedule,
www.YogiMuse.com

You can follow her on Facebook:
Michelle Marchildon, The Yogi Muse,
and on Twitter: where she's more clever and concise,
at Michelle_Muse.

Theme Weaver: The Workshop

Michelle offers a weekend workshop to bring virtue to life for your students. *Theme Weaver: Connecting the Power of Inspiration to Your Yoga Teaching*, instills the concepts of the *Other Eight Limbed Path*.

In addition to yoga, Michelle is a motivational speaker on how to bring more into your life, at any time, starting with any circumstance. She teaches *asana* workshops and offers yoga retreats wherever she doesn't have to make dinner.

For more information, her schedule, the blog and to contact her, please go to *www.YogiMuse.com*

Theme Weaver Journal and Workbook Coming Soon!

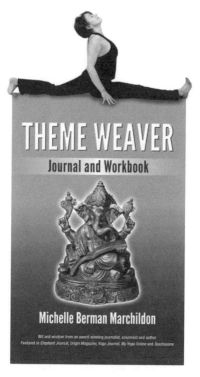

How many times have you had a wonderful idea to use
in a class only to lose it when you needed it later?

Now there is a place to keep everything together
for your teaching.

Look for the companion book to **Theme Weaver: Connect
the Power of Inspiration to Teaching Yoga** coming soon.

This unique workbook will have practice pages for creating
your Mission Statement and unique Yoga Brand, finding
your themes, contemplations and storing theme worksheets.

As you grow and evolve your teaching, your work will be in
one place so that no effort is ever wasted—or lost.
You are welcome! Namaste.